# The
# Contented
# Mother's
# Guide

GHP

# The
# Contented
# Mother's
# Guide

## Essential advice to help you be a
## happy, calm and confident mother

# Gina Ford

## GHP

**Vermilion**
**LONDON**

1 3 5 7 9 10 8 6 4 2

Published in 2012 by Vermilion, an imprint of Ebury Publishing
Ebury Publishing is a Random House Group company

The Random House Group Limited Reg. No. 954009
Addresses for companies within the Random House Group can be found at
www.randomhouse.co.uk

A CIP catalogue record for this book is available from the British Library

The Random House Group Limited supports The Forest Stewardship Council
(FSC®), the leading international forest certification organisation. Our books carrying the FSC label are printed on FSC® certified paper. FSC is the only forest
certification scheme endorsed by the leading environmental organisations, including
Greenpeace. Our paper procurement policy can be found at
www.randomhouse.co.uk/environment

Printed and bound by CPI Group (UK) Ltd, Croydon, CR0 4YY

ISBN 9780091912710

Copies are available at special rates for bulk orders. Contact the sales development
team on 020 7840 8487 for more information.

To buy books by your favourite authors and register for offers, visit
www.randomhouse.co.uk

The information in this book has been compiled by way of general guidance in
relation to the specific subjects addressed, but is not a substitute and not to be
relied on for medical, healthcare, pharmaceutical or other professional advice on
specific circumstances and in specific locations. Please consult your GP before
changing, stopping or starting any medical treatment. So far as the author is
aware the information given is correct and up to date as at September 2011.
Practice, laws and regulations all change, and the reader should obtain up-to-date
professional advice on any such issues. The author and publishers disclaim, as far
as the law allows, any liability arising directly or indirectly from the use, or misuse,
of the information contained in this book.

*To my beloved mother*

# Contents

# Contents

# Acknowledgements

I would like to express my gratitude to all the mums on my online community and the mums I have worked with over the years, who have helped with their advice and experiences on motherhood.

I would also like to thank my publisher Fiona MacIntyre and editor Louise Francis for their constant encouragement and faith in my work, and thanks to the rest of the team at Vermilion for all their hard work on the book.

Special thanks are also owed to my agent Emma Kirby, for her dedication and support, and to Laura Simmons, for her efforts in gathering information for the book. Thank you to Kate Brian, the website editor of Contentedbaby.com, Alison Jermyn, Jane Waygood, Peter Ritchie and Rory Jenkins, and the rest of the team at Contentedbaby.com, for their support while I was writing this book and their wonderful work on the website.

And, finally, I am ever grateful for the huge support I receive from the thousands of readers of my books who take the time to contact me – a huge thank you to you all and much love to your contented babies.

You painted no Madonnas
On chapel walls in Rome;
But with a touch diviner
You lived one in your home.
You wrote no lofty poems
That critics counted art;
But with a nobler vision,
You lived them in your heart.

You carved no shapeless marble
To some high soul design
But with a finer sculpture
You shaped this soul of mine.
You built no great cathedrals
That centuries applaud;
But with a grace exquisite
Your life cathedraled God.
Had I the gift of Raphael
Or Michelangelo
O what a rare Madonna
My mother's life would show.

*Thomas Fessenden*

# Introduction

There is no greater life-changing experience than becoming a mother. When we go through any kind of change, we look for guidance and support, and the best people to advise us are often those who have been through the same experience themselves. That's why in this book I am, for the most part, handing over to the mothers – the wonderful community of mums on the Contented Baby website, who have shared their experiences of motherhood with me. Most have followed the routines and advice in my *Contented Little Baby* books, and have kindly given me their feedback and told me what did and didn't work for them. I call them my CLB mums!

My community of mothers is often experiencing pregnancy for the second (and sometimes third or fourth!) time, and their depth of experience, and generous support of each other, is rich with reassurance and advice. Like a chat with a group of best friends, giving thoughtful and funny opinions, it is hard not to leave the discussions feeling upbeat and reassured. These conversations from mum to mum have provided such a wealth of fantastic information that I just had to share them with you. In this indispensable guide, I have worked with the mums to distil the best advice on being a contented mother. The result is this one-stop guide that will help you to navigate all the essential issues of motherhood.

With refreshing honesty, the CLB mums share the highs and the lows of that roller-coaster first year. This book focuses on the key issues that stood out for them – both practical and emotional; all the everyday challenges and common concerns that you're likely to face as a new mum. In addition to the advice from the CLB community is my own guidance, based on the many years I worked with families, looking after young babies and advising and helping new parents. One thing that you will learn is that there is seldom one perfect way to tackle problems you might face – you just have to find the right way for you and your baby. With the personal experiences of hundreds of mothers, *The Contented Mother's Guide* will help you to make the best choices and fully embrace your new role as a mother.

I know more than anyone how important it is to have a contented baby and have helped millions of mothers to achieve this. But what is just as important is for you to be contented too. It's essential to make sure that your own needs are met – because if you're a contented and happy mother, there's a much greater chance that your baby will be contented and happy too.

If you would like to share your own experience and join our fantastic community of mums, please do come and join us on the Contented Baby website – www.contentedbaby.com.

Good luck and warmest wishes

Gina

# 1

# Looking After Yourself

Very few women are truly prepared for life with their first baby, and you can see from the pages that follow that those early months especially involve a big adjustment in your life. Exhaustion can lead to negative feelings about the way you are coping, but it's reassuring to know that you are not alone, which is the reason I've included this subject in the book.

A few months down the line, when your little one is sleeping for longer periods and a routine is established, many – probably most – mums have periods when they feel bored with the constant round of repetitive tasks necessary to bring up children. Sometimes boredom can lead to feelings of frustration, resentment and even anger, which are heightened if you're fairly isolated and don't have the company of other adults for much of the day. It's hard not to feel guilty about these thoughts, and the mums who've contributed to these pages are brave to admit to their feelings.

In this book, I want to show that it's normal to feel this way, but also that there are things you can do about it. Firstly, you need to carve a little time out for yourself each day. As mum Gill says, 'Your needs will no longer come first – but make sure they are still on the list and not ignored completely. It is important to recognise that this is not being selfish. No matter what job someone is doing, they need time away from it.'

Here we've got some great ideas for how to create 'me-time' that also emphasise its importance. If you can't bring yourself to prioritise your own pleasure and self-development, take a tip from mum Linda, who says it's important for the children to 'realise that there are times in the day when Mummy chooses something for herself'. Now you can justify restarting your hobby – it's good for the children, too! Linda adds, 'Remember, you are not selfish in trying to have "me-time". It is an essential element in your life, helping to ensure your happiness, health and ability to be a good mum.'

You can also see how important the occasional night out is, as are friends – new and old. And finally, the CLB mums have contributed some great tips on how to get organised in the housework department, so that you feel less swamped by your 'to do' list.

## Dealing with negative feelings

You've waited so many months for this baby to arrive and now you feel miserable and sometimes as if you can't cope at all. Everyone says, 'Oooh, it's all worth it,' and you're thinking,

'When?!' Does this sound familiar? Do not fear; negative feelings are common at this early stage. After a few weeks your hormones sort themselves out, you will grow in confidence and you'll start to enjoy your baby more.

## Mums' Top Tips

❀ 'I think it is normal to feel lost in the early days of motherhood – you become so much mother and wife that you lose the essence of you. But it is still there, you are still there, underneath the (manky but practical) trackies.' **Tanya**

❀ 'The first three months are so very, very hard. It would have helped me if I had known that everyone seems to find it so difficult, as I felt very alone in my feelings of claustrophobia and helplessness in the first few weeks. I was also shocked at how difficult my relationship with my husband became.' **Becky**

❀ 'It does get better and easier. My baby is now eight-and-a-half months and, thanks to Gina, she sleeps 7pm–7.30am with few disturbances.' **Lenita**

❀ 'One of my friends was really supportive when I went into shock at the sheer awfulness of the first few weeks of motherhood, and she called it the Hundred Days of Hell. She promised me that by the end of 100 days, things wouldn't be so bad. And of course, they're not. I think doing the CLB routines makes it much, much easier in the long run and once your baby starts smiling and giggling, at least you do get something back.' **Celia**

❀ 'I would say that weeks seven to ten are the worst, then things start calming down. Try to tell your husband how you feel, or if you can't find the words, write it down. Somehow, just admitting to someone else how awful you feel can help. If you have a sympathetic health visitor or GP, talk to them. Another piece of advice that helped me was to split the day into blocks and then you can at least feel you've had one good part of the day. Gradually you'll be noticing more good blocks than bad and then more good days than bad, and you'll be through the other side. Being a mum has been the hardest thing I have ever done in my life.' **Fee**

## ■ Mum-to-Mum: *Coping with the monotony*

### Query

*'I am really bored at the moment. I feel that my days are filled with washing, cooking, cleaning, entertaining – and nothing else. I love my daughter to bits, and I know I wouldn't want to do anything else, but I have been finding the past few days and weeks very difficult. I don't think the dark winter days help. I*

*just keep thinking back to the time when I had a life that didn't solely revolve around the house. Can anyone help?'* **Claire**

## Answers

'Try to find a few hobbies to do at home. I make things out of Fimo, draw very occasionally, knit, sew and play guitar. I never have time, but they are there for backup. It's so easy to go one-track "house/child" brained!' **Gwen**

'I often feel sadly unfulfilled by my role as a mother. I am just trying to make the most of this time in my daughter's life and give her the best start and hopefully I will pick up some part of my life again. I have a master plan that involves a huge career change. I just need something exciting to think about and dream about other than this family and this house. You could formulate a plan for getting some excitement into your life again!' **Fee**

'Remember the highs and try to get through the lows. I have to try to remember that there are people worse off. I have just bought my son a pair of waterproof trousers, so even if it's wet I am going to the park to get out. I have to remember at times like this that I am lucky as it's all I ever wanted – to have a baby and a family, etc. Usually we go to the park a couple of times a week for the swings or just a run around. I now even go to the local garden centre to let him get out and about there!' **Nicola**

'Even if you just worked one day a week (if you do the sort of job that would accommodate that) it might help, and you'd get your daughter's face lighting up to see you at the end of the day.' **Becky**

'Love what you have chosen to do. Allow yourself to be encouraged by individuals who have achieved great things while still being a great parent. Let these wonderful mums and dads become your inspiration. Or choose a person you know, or someone well known, who is living the life you are dreaming of. I know someone who has set her sights on writing a book. She has allocated herself an hour each night to work on it. She knows that it will take a long time, but the satisfaction of doing it is immense. You may need to organise your life to fit this in, but you will feel huge satisfaction when you achieve your goals.' **Maria**

'Take any offers you are given, whether it is washing-up, cooking a meal or taking baby out for a couple of hours, to give you a break. It took me a while to realise that I wasn't going to lose the supermum title just because I left my boy with someone else for a couple of hours so I could go swimming. I felt better for having time out, and it made me appreciate him all the more.' **Debbie**

'Find a babysitter one morning a week or consider a reciprocal arrangement with another mum. Resist the temptation to cook or do something useful in this slot! This constructed time is for you to relax or have fun. You could do an exercise class, or enrol in a vocational course or something practical. The subject is not that important; the main thing is you are doing something for you. Something as simple as shopping or having a haircut in peace can give you an enormous boost.' **Gill**

'I went along to my postnatal group. It was great to chat to other mothers at the same stage, and I learnt a lot from them. It also got me out of the house, which is so important; feeling isolated can be devastating for new mums. Later I searched on the internet for mother-and-baby activities in my area and, as a result, I enrolled for gym-babes, swimming and sing and sign. It has been brilliant as I have met lots of other mums. Go and get out there – both you and your little one will benefit so much, as babies love the social side of life just as much as their mums.' **Kelly**

**Gina says**: As the CLB mums have advised, it is important to find time to do the things you enjoy and, most importantly, get out of the house or have other mums round for adult company. Remember, it's okay – even essential – to sometimes let the housework slip and indulge yourself with some more interesting activities. Your wellbeing is much more important than a spotlessly clean house.

# Making time for yourself

Try to take care of yourself. People ask me why I include advice in my routines about eating and drinking. It's because most new mums put themselves at the bottom of the list of priorities. It can be 4pm before some mums realise they've only had a cup of tea and half a piece of toast all day. Make sure you eat a good balanced diet and that you are sitting down regularly to eat – it's no good having a banana for breakfast and a big dinner but nothing in between.

Sleep is a valuable time out! In the early days, try to sleep when your little one sleeps. CLB mum Emma says, 'With practice, you can soon learn to catnap. I used to go back to bed at 8.30am and then again during my baby's lunchtime nap. Looking back, it absolutely kept me sane in those early, sleep-deprived days.'

If you are breastfeeding, it is a very good idea to express the 10pm feed earlier in the day. This may take a little time and organisation, but if you are disciplined, it means the 10pm feed can be done by your partner, giving you at least an hour to yourself in the evening for a long soak in the bath, or any other form of relaxation, such as reading or emailing a friend. Many mothers find themselves tired and desperate for a break at this time in the day, which can, in turn, have an adverse affect on their milk supply. This arrangement also gives your partner a chance to have his own bonding time with baby, which is so important. Many times, I have come across two parents fussing unnecessarily over a baby, when the attention of one would be sufficient, thereby releasing the other to do something else, or simply enjoy being 'off-duty' for a short time. If your baby is bottle-fed, then it is even simpler for you to get into the routine of letting your partner offer the 10pm feed.

## Mums' Top Tips

❁ 'Let your children see you reading a book or the news-paper, so they realise that there are times in the day when Mummy chooses something for herself. I always made a point of reading the paper while they watched a short TV programme after lunch. It is also good for chil-dren to see you doing the household jobs, rather than you trying to fit them all in while they are at nursery or asleep. As soon as they are old enough, offer them a duster or a little broom and let them help. Remember, you are not selfish in trying to have "me-time". It is an essential element in your life, helping to ensure your happiness, health and ability to be a good mum.' **Linda**

❁ 'The key to finding a way out of the "lack of energy and time" rut is to be realistic about the situation you are facing, and valuing quality over quantity. This may sound obvious, but it is easy to get caught up in what "should" be happening instead of what "could" be happening. Get into the habit of looking after yourself, and don't give up after a bad day.' **Maria**

❀ 'Planning is what is required to make sure you spend time away from the family each week. Join a yoga class and pay your course fee upfront to make sure you go; or arrange a time each week or fortnight to meet your girl-friends for coffee or dinner. If you know when your special time is going to be, you will be more likely to keep the date with yourself – and feel a million times better for it.' **Kim**

❀ 'My husband and I agreed that we would have one night a week each as an activity night. My husband has Monday night and I have Thursday night, to go out and do what we each enjoy doing. Often we use it to keep in contact with our friends – and this also gives us some-thing else to talk (and gossip!) about.' **Debbie**

❀ 'I have a night out with girlfriends about once every month or six weeks, and this is a great opportunity to chat and catch up without the kids running around. My husband and I also try to get out together every couple of months. This is undoubtedly made easier by having my parents living nearby, but even without this support, it would still be worth making the effort.' **Claire**

✿ 'Increase your support network by joining a parenting website. Contentedbaby.com was the perfect choice for me. I have gained a lot of knowledge and confidence and made many new friends.' **Kelly**

✿ 'Go for dinner and talk about something other than baby – work, friends, holidays or what's in the news. Go to the cinema and talk about the film afterwards. Go bowling, so you can laugh about how hopeless you are! Just make an effort to enjoy some couple time. It will do both of you the world of good to remember that you are people, and not just parents. Yes, life has changed, but try to keep some of the old life as well, as one day you will have that back.' **Debbie**

## ■ Mum-to-Mum: *Feeling guilty*

### Query

*'I've noticed that I'm spending less and less time actually playing with my children. I start each day with good intentions, then end up running around with the vacuum or having to spend time cooking for them. I feel so awful when people say, "Ooh, you are such a supermum, coping with three children so young," when I know that they spend quite a bit of time playing on their own or watching TV. I need some top tips, please!'* **Julie**

## Answers

'Currently I spend about 20 minutes solid playing in the morning, then in the afternoon it's either an outing (is that playing?) or just in the house, where I keep them busy doing something. However, all day long they are always with me, talking to me, watching me, so although it's not playing, it's still interacting and they are learning. When I'm doing chores I try to involve them or turn it into a game, e.g. they love me vacuuming as I pretend to catch them and they like the suction feeling on their feet. Remember it's good for them to create and think up their own games too.' **Anna**

'While I was trying to get ahead with planning I found a link on the CLB site to the FlyLady website (see page 199) that I found very useful. I've signed up for their emails and it's helped me get a better routine going, which in turn is giving me more time to think about what I want to do with the children.' **Polly**

**Gina says:** Don't be too hard on yourself and remember no one is a 'supermum'. I liked Kim's approach: 'My house is pretty clean, the family is well enough nourished – there's at least a block of cheese and a loaf of bread in the cupboard, and I usually manage to get my son out of his pyjamas and the bed made. To me this is coping and anything more than this is a bonus!'

**CLB Mums' Top 10 Best Ways ... to
Save Time on Chores**

1. Be organised. Each week, I make a list of what I have to do, what I want to do and the week's 'horrible job' (e.g. cleaning the oven). Just the process of setting everything out makes the situation more manageable.

2. Do a massive cook and freeze. Once a month on a Sunday, my husband takes the girls out for the afternoon and leaves me at home to cook. I then freeze the results in double portions and make sure there are lots of vegetables in each. It is very labour-intensive, but it is definitely the best way.

3. Combine housework and playtime. I usually plan extra time to change my duvet cover, as it usually involves a game where my children and I all play monsters in the bed. This can break the monotony of cleaning for you and give you a chance to laugh with your children.

4. Get rid of the clutter. The less you have, the easier it will be to keep your house clean and tidy. So, get rid of stuff! Be ruthless. Recycle. Have a sale of unwanted baby equipment. Give to charity.

5. I do the cleaning in short 15-minute bursts and set the timer when I do it. It really makes a difference – you get much more done in a very short time and you can focus on just getting one bit of a room really clean.

6. Whenever I leave a room, I always take something with me which should go into the next room I am going to. Also, never go upstairs or downstairs without something in your hand. It's amazing how much stuff ends up in the wrong place and how much difference it makes!

7. Don't iron! It's such a waste of time. I buy clothes that don't need ironing, or hang clothes on the line so that more often than not they don't need ironing. My husband irons his own shirts.

8. I put a load in the washer as I'm going to bed and then in the morning I can hang the clothes straight out and put the next load in, so I can get two loads done before breakfast.

9. I find that I get loads of cleaning done if I do it in the evening for an hour or so while listening to music on my iPod. It's really relaxing and you don't notice the work that you're doing. It's great for ironing and any kind of tidying up.

10. I try to get up an hour early once a week to get things done that I never normally find any time for. It's amazing how much you can get done when the house is quiet and everyone else is asleep. Of course, it's a pain when you're dragging yourself out of bed, but afterwards I'm always so pleased with what I've managed to achieve that it makes it all worthwhile.

## Summary – points to remember

- Feeling exhausted and overwhelmed in the early days of your baby's life is normal. Don't think that you're the only new mum not coping admirably; like you, other new parents like to give a cool, calm and collected illusion in public!

- Ups, downs and negative thoughts are totally normal. Share your feelings with a sympathetic friend – or your health visitor or GP.

- Being a mum may be what you always wanted, but it's common to find the repetitive tasks of caring for children boring at times. Creating 'me-time' can alleviate this.

- Take time to nurture yourself so that you, in turn, can nurture others. Looking after yourself is *not* being selfish.

- Plan your 'me-time', treat it with respect and be organised. Creating time, and finding interesting ways to fill it, won't happen by itself.

- Treat your 'appointment with yourself' in the same way as you would any other appointment. Try not to let it slip. You wouldn't readily let down your hairdresser, friend or boss, so why let yourself down?

- Accept all offers of help and support. This won't diminish your role as a mother; it will just help you to do the job better.

- Once you have created some precious 'me-time', don't be tempted to fill it with useful jobs!

- Friends play an important part in keeping you feeling positive. Take steps to meet other new mums – in person or online. Remember that your partner is your friend, too!

- Batch-cooking, online shopping and planning your household chores can all help to save you time for relaxation and other interests. If you are in the position, consider employing a cleaner, even just once a month.

- Less clutter saves you time; there is less to clean, tidy and fall over, and it is easier to find things.

# 2

# Getting Back in Shape

Like most new mums, you may be worried about when you'll return to your pre-pregnancy weight and shape. You will no doubt have become much more home-based since your baby arrived, and it's hard to resist temptation when food is constantly to hand. Reduced sleep can also make the energy boost of sugary or fatty snacks even trickier to avoid. In addition, we're subjected to a daily gallery in the press and on TV of celebrity mums who are back to their bikini weights within weeks of giving birth. These images are guaranteed to make any normal woman feel bad!

The truth is that very gradual weight loss is best, and that means harnessing your willpower and adopting a long-term healthy-eating plan. However, remember that breastfeeding mums, especially, should never drastically reduce their calorie intake, and it is particularly important to eat extra calcium- and iron-rich foods during these months. Dairy products are one of the best forms of calcium and green leafy vegetables will give you a good intake of iron.

In this chapter, the CLB mums and some health and

fitness experts offer bite-sized chunks of great advice based on personal experience. Some suggestions are to increase your fitness with very little outlay by using exercise DVDs (borrowing them from the library is a good way to try before you buy), getting out and about with the buggy or using an online running programme such as 'The Couch to 5K' (see page 199). Some mums recommend diet clubs, such as Weight Watchers, many of which have programmes you can follow online if you're not able to get out to meetings.

We've also got some great tips for looking good, from improving your posture to mum Laura's secret weapon – control pants – which 'give the illusion of a childfree waist-line'! Perhaps one of the most important points to remember is not to be too hard on yourself – yes, you want to get back in shape, but give yourself time. With a little perseverance and willpower, you will get there in the end.

## Establishing an exercise routine

After the arrival of your baby, it is good to start thinking about your health and fitness, but don't beat yourself up for recovering gradually from childbirth and not hitting the gym four times per week. In common with a lot of busy mothers, you may find it difficult to make time to exercise. The best way to establish a regular exercise routine is to make an appointment with yourself on a routine basis, even if it's only 20 minutes, three times a week. Write your goals down on a planner, and then try to stick to the weekly minimum. If you're not too disciplined, consider getting a personal trainer – you could even ask for sessions as a 'new mum' gift.

CLB mum Kim says, 'I booked a session with a personal trainer and outlined what I would like to achieve. He then helped me to make a weekly plan, which includes the days I should exercise on and what exercises I should do. I find it helps to be organised in this way, rather than dragging myself off the sofa when I feel I must get fit. When I know what days I'm exercising, I can also plan my meals accordingly, so I'm not filling up on a large meal at the wrong time. I also find I keep to the regime much better if I have obtainable goals to work towards.'

Fitness expert Gill Macaulay says the key is to find a variety of ways to fit exercise into your life: 'Make it a daily challenge to find ways to move and work your body. Climb stairs rather than use escalators or lifts; walk your dog; chase your kids; mow the lawn; and walk rather than drive, if you can. Anything that moves your limbs is not only working on your strength and fitness, but it's a stress-buster too. Think about moving in small ways and the effort will soon add up.'

If you can't find time to get out of the house, try using workout DVDs. This way you can exercise in the comfort of your own home whenever it suits you. If you've only recently given birth, buy a postnatal workout DVD that will help you get back into exercising, without exhausting you so much that you're too tired to look after your baby. If you have older children, choose one that contains workouts of different lengths that you can combine, or do separately, depending on how much time you have.

## Mums' Top Tips

❀ 'When I can't get out of the house, I put on really good disco/dance music and dance my socks off for 30 minutes. Of course, having a hugely entertained baby watching me go mad has made it easier!' **Erika**

❀ 'Set realistic goals and get friends involved to help keep you motivated.' **Justine**

❀ 'A 10-minute walk every day is good for your sanity! Even if you don't feel up to negotiating shop doorways and aisles with your buggy, just getting out and window shop-ping will help prevent cabin fever – and if you have a park or beach nearby, even better.' **Debbie**

❀ 'Treat exercise as "me-time"; after all, you're doing some-thing that will give you more energy and make you look and feel good. If you're attending a class, it's also a chance to meet new people in an environment that has nothing to do with babies. So, make your arrangements, try to stick to them and enjoy!' **Susie**

✿ 'Spend one evening a week at an exercise class. If it's a regular arrangement, then you're less likely to find an excuse not to go. Think of it as a proper evening off!' **Laura**

✿ 'I rejoined the gym. With a little effort, you can begin to see results pretty quickly and this, in turn, helps me to eat healthily.' **Miranda**

✿ 'I've started swimming three times a week. I get to the pool for opening at 7am and I am home in time for my husband to leave for work. The morning works better for me, as by the evening I am shattered and not in the mood for exercise at all. It has transformed my shape like no exercise I have ever done.' **Claire**

✿ 'Decide when you are going to exercise and stick to it. Make it clear to your partner that he will be responsible for your baby at those times. Otherwise, you will be forever trying to fit it in, and it will be too easy to convince yourself that you don't have the time. This will have a negative effect not only on your fitness, but on your wellbeing.' **Susie**

# ▉ Mum-to-Mum: *Getting in shape*

## Query

*'I am tired of feeling unfit and flabby! My son is four months old and I've stopped breastfeeding now so I have no excuse not to exercise. Any fitness tips?'* **Laura**

## Answers

'How about trying walking or a workout with a stability ball? You could also look for a postnatal exercise class in your area, such as Babyfit. For motivation, take a photo of yourself now in your underwear, revealing any slightly wobbly bits from both the front and side views. Produce some copies and put them where you normally relax and eat. Harsh, but effective!' **Emily**

'Why don't you treat yourself to a mini trampoline? They are not too expensive and are fun – you can bounce while watching TV!' **Susie**

'I hate exercise that takes too long and gets few results. I used to do a programme called Body-*for*-LIFE (see page 199) and I achieved amazing results in three months – I was toned and lean. I loved it because it was 20 minutes of cardio work three days a week, and 45 minutes of weights three days a week. It's interval training, and if you like that sort of thing, it may be for you.' **Cathy**

'I'm quite lazy, and so never manage to follow a plan involving exercise at home. Group classes are the best motivator for me.' **Erika**

'I have been running on a "Cool Running" programme called "The Couch to 5K" (see page 199). I'm on week five now, and it's all going well. When I first started, my knees weren't great, but now they barely give me any problems. They are getting stronger from muscles I am developing through running. Even more importantly, my energy levels have risen, my tolerance has increased and my mood is so much more upbeat.' **Amy**

'I've started cycling – it's fabulous and my daughter adores it. Once little ones reach 9 kg they can sit on a seat on the back of the bike. Eva would stay there all day. She even sleeps while she's in it! It's the only way that we really travel at the moment. I can't get enough of it – and it reduces our carbon footprint!' **Emma**

**Gina says:** It is good for you physically and emotionally to start getting in shape, but there are several pitfalls to be avoided when exercising in the first five months after having a baby. Fitness consultant Judy Di Fiores says, 'New mothers should avoid high-impact work (such as strenuous aerobic classes or jogging on hard ground) and remember that the joints are vulnerable. Pilates, swimming, stationary cycling and walking are all good low-impact sports, but ideally you should attend a specialist postnatal class. Such classes can be found on the website for The Guild of Pregnancy and Postnatal Exercise Instructors (see page 199). It is also important for new mothers to learn how to build up their core strength, address postural changes, tone up their stomach muscles and become more aware of their posture. One simple piece of advice is to draw in the tummy as you are walking, in order to support your back. Often mothers will push their buggy in a way that limits the fitness benefit and may cause backache. When walking up hills, for example, many mothers tend to bend forwards to push the buggy up the hill. I would advise keeping your back straight and rolling your shoulders down your back, so that the legs take the strain. Wrists should be parallel to the floor. This is definitely more of a workout and, even better, one that you don't need to plan or think about.'

## Looking good

Pregnancy certainly puts a strain on your body and it will be some months before you look and feel your old self. One of the cheapest and easiest things you can do for your appearance is to think about posture. Fitness expert Gill Macaulay says, 'Poor posture has a significant effect on health and the way we look. Not only can it make us look older, but it can also lead to an enlarged tummy, double chin, curved spine, backache and potential internal problems. So, when you're on your feet, stand straight with your weight evenly balanced, your shoulders relaxed and down, and your chin level. When sitting, try to keep your back straight and long by engaging your abdominal muscles and rolling your shoulders down and away from your neck. Be conscious of your position when you are lifting your child or pushing the buggy. It won't necessarily feel easy or comfortable to make changes, as you may be adjusting the habits of a lifetime, but the health benefits of good posture are both visible and invisible. If you feel this is something you would like to work on, then yoga, Pilates, ballet and the Alexander Technique can all help to tone muscles and improve posture.'

## Making time for you

Once you have a baby, the indulgent two-hour preparation for an evening out becomes a distant memory. The biggest secret to looking good in record time, however, is to prepare beforehand. If you already have good baby routines in place, you should find this possible, as you can work your preparation around your daily schedule. CLB mum Briony says, 'If you have a night out coming up, plan what you want to wear in advance, and try it on. Make sure you also include underwear, accessories and shoes, or it's certain that what you need will be lost in the laundry, or hidden at the back of the wardrobe. The early evening is a hectic point in any family day, so don't expect to be able to feed your baby, prepare for a babysitter and paint your nails all at the same time. Think about having a shower, giving yourself a manicure or shaving your legs earlier in the day, when you will be less pressurised. The less you leave until the last moment, the better your chances of being able to walk out of the door feeling relaxed and looking good – and the more likely you are to have a good evening.'

## Mums' Top Tips

❀ 'My tip for looking good can be summed up in two words: control pants! The skin on my tummy has never recovered from carrying my second baby, who weighed an eye-watering 10 lb 3 oz. Despite recovering my pre-pregnancy weight, I am far from my pre-pregnancy shape, and haven't the time or the inclination to do 100 sit-ups a day. Control pants give the illusion of a childfree waistline – and only your partner need know the truth!' **Laura**

❀ 'Water is not a great friend for our hands, and as new mums we wash our hands constantly. To stop your hands ageing, use hand cream regularly. Put a pot of cream next to the kitchen sink, another in the bathroom, one by the changing mat, and one in your car.' **Megan**

❧ 'No matter how tempting it might be to fall into bed with-out cleaning your face, don't do it; your skin will appreciate it if you remove all traces of make-up and apply your mois-turiser before going to bed. If you are short of time or beauty products, baby wipes can be used as a fast and inexpensive way to remove make-up.' **Gill**

## CLB Mums' Top 10 Best Ways … to Lose Weight

1. Cut out all alcohol. Drinking booze was seriously having the biggest impact on me not losing weight. Since I kicked booze it has been much easier.

2. Do loads of exercise. The benefits of exercise are great! It gives you more energy in the long run and makes you feel better about yourself and I am totally convinced it makes me more interested in sex! I do an exercise DVD with the kids around and they love it.

3. Gradually eat more healthily, reduce portion sizes, have a cup of soup and fruit and oatcakes when you feel hungry. Eating three meals a day and making breakfast big worked for me. I have found I have better energy levels and just feel a lot better for eating a big breakfast.

4. Don't expect changes overnight and find a dieting buddy – I have one online who has spurred me on a lot!

5. To motivate you, keep a pair of jeans you have been dying to get into again on display. When I finally put mine on again I nearly fainted with happiness!

6. I think it is all about balance. I combined Slimming World ideas with Gillian McKeith's *You Are What You Eat* and with just general sensible eating. For about a year now I have been eating really healthily and exercising regularly. Make up your own version of how you want it to work and you'll do just fine.

7. Go to Weight Watchers (see page 200). I lost a steady 2 lb a week just by eating healthily and limiting myself to one small bag of Maltesers a day, as I'm a chocoholic! Keep persevering and don't expect too much weight loss too quickly.

8. Try the GI diet – it's the only one that has ever worked for me. It involves changing the way you eat, rather than just cutting out or cutting back. It also didn't involve me being hungry. I lost one-and-a-half stones in about four months.

9. I found out that if you don't drink enough water your metabolism slows down by 3 per cent, which apparently is about 45 calories or something just for not drinking enough.

10. Give yourself a break! Unless you're an A-lister who has a nude scene to do in the next blockbuster Hollywood film and with access to nannies, personal trainers, cleaners, chefs, chauffeurs and personal shoppers, there is going to be a limit to your capabilities!

## Summary – points to remember

● Your health and fitness are very important – and looking after yourself means you're better able to look after your children.

● When it comes to exercise, the key is to choose a sport or activity that you enjoy and that suits you. If you try to persevere with an activity you dislike, you won't stick to your plan for long. By looking forward to something, you are much more likely to keep it up and feel the benefits.

● Walking is one of the cheapest and easiest forms of exercise, and it is good for you and your children.

● Booking and paying for exercise classes in advance is a good incentive to go.

● Don't beat yourself up if you stray from the plan. Any exercise is better than nothing, and you can get back on course as soon as you become organised again. A routine is important, but try to stay flexible to avoid feeling too frustrated.

● Try not to compare your child, domestic arrangements or exercise plan with anyone else's; work out what is right for you and your circumstances.

● If you are having a bad week and all your plans go 'belly-up', try not to see it as a long-term catastrophe. Accept that your arrangements – or your new diet – will fall by the wayside sometimes, but just get back on track the following week without fretting too much over what went wrong.

● Whether you are dealing with domestic arrangements, a fitness regime or a beauty schedule, always try to set yourself realistic goals. It is always better to add to a programme, rather than feeling that you have failed to meet your initial goals.

- If mum isn't happy, no one is. It's hard to raise a happy baby, or nurture anyone if you are on the edge. Be proud. Being a parent is the most important job. But to do it well you must also look after yourself.

- Remember, small and simple steps can bring about significant changes.

# 3
# Relationships

Becoming a parent is a truly life-changing moment for both you and your partner. Overnight, you change from being a couple to being a family. You are no longer a wife or girl-friend alone, but a mother too; your partner becomes a father; parents and in-laws become grandparents. With all these changes, there is joy and excitement at the opportunities the new roles bring, but there are also plenty of potential problems along the way, as individuals adjust to the arrival of this precious new life. Your new baby may be the fulfilment of a dream, but the sleepless nights, financial pressures, lifestyle restrictions and never-ending chores can test the strongest of relationships. In addition, relationships with friends, particularly those without children, can be chal-lenged, as can connections with parents and in-laws. With time and effort, however, these relationships can also be enhanced, and often couples feel closer to one another, and to their extended family, after the arrival of a baby.

In this chapter, using the experiences of the mothers from the Contentedbaby.com online community, we will look at some of the most common conflicts and how other people have dealt with the issues that confronted them. Just as children grow and develop, your relationships too have to adapt and keep up. It is not always an easy ride.

Relationships with other family members can be affected as everyone becomes an 'expert' parent, offering usually unwanted advice. CLB mum Debbie found that as her son Max got older and started to develop his own personality, everyone had an opinion as to how to help him along. She said, 'Sometimes an outside perspective is good, and the advice can be sound, but use only what you want and disregard the rest. You don't have to be confrontational; I just smile, agree it's a good idea and then say how I plan to adapt it. You are the one who is with your baby the most, so it's your teaching that will help him grow – and consistency is the key.'

As you adjust to parenthood, there is bound to be a strain on your relationship and many couples find themselves arguing seriously for the first time, but knowing that you are not alone in what you are experiencing can be a huge comfort. Taking advice and support from others who have travelled the same road will help you to ride the bumps and emerge all the stronger and happier from your journey. In this chapter, Fee shares her very personal story about her marriage difficulties and receives some invaluable advice from other mums.

In those tough early days, remind yourselves that the first three or four months are the hardest it's ever going to be. As your baby gets bigger and your routine becomes second nature, life will get much easier and relationships will improve all round. Until then, try to put your inevitable tensions aside and enjoy these precious weeks, with their host of magical milestones, together as a family. To get off to a good start with friends and relatives, limit visitors to times when you really are up to seeing them. Mum Emma says: 'Limit visitors to immediate family in the time straight after the birth, and if they are happy to stay outside of your home, so much the better. The best thing for me was that my mum came to stay for as long as I needed her. She was unobtrusive and simply helped out around the house. Most importantly, she only offered advice when asked!'

## Advice from others

Having a baby can bring the family closer together but also cause tensions, especially if family members, often your own parents or in-laws, have a different approach to baby-care. But CLB mum Gill found that things actually changed for the better with her mother-in-law once the baby was born: 'My mother-in-law came to help after the arrival of our daughter. When the baby was asleep, we would sit down for coffee and a chat, and I was astonished to learn things about her that I had never known before. We talked about her childhood, her ambitions and her feelings when she met my father-in-law. I started to see her in a different light – as a friend and individual – rather than simply as "my husband's mum", and this was a lovely development.' It is important to be flexible with older relatives and try to see things from their point of view. Remember that they have a lifetime's experience that may be useful or worth listening to. We all like to think we know best, but try not to dismiss people's ideas simply because they differ from yours. We can all be stubborn at times, but it is important to put individual feelings aside for the sake of your family, not least for your child who will have their own relationship with that person.

If there are difficulties, try to handle them sensitively and consider your partner's feelings and predicament when a disagreement involves his relatives. One mum shared her own experience: 'When our first baby was born, I felt like my in-laws were trying to take over. They were always dropping round and telling me what to do. I got really frustrated and asked my husband to speak to them. For a while afterwards, things were very frosty and we hardly saw them. Looking back, I know they were only trying to help and I should have talked to them direct about my feelings, rather than forming a triangle with my poor husband stuck in the middle. Things are better now, thankfully, as we have all relaxed a little. But had I just been brave enough to say something in the first place, it would have been better.'

## ■ Mum-to-Mum: *Mother-in-law issues*

### Query

*'It drives me to distraction when my mother-in-law deliberately ignores our schedule. We picked our son up just before 10pm and found that not only had my in-laws kept him up all night, but they had also fed him the emergency bottle "because he was crying and needed it". I really don't want to deprive my in-laws from looking after our baby, but I also want them to respect our wishes. Any suggestions?'* **Penny**

### Answers

'I've always made it clear that if either set of grandparents want to be involved in caring for my kids, then they have to follow my rules! I'm the one who's got to deal with the fall-out if they don't. To get round this, I type out full instructions, as well as a "trouble-shooting" guide, and give it to them each time they babysit. I ask them to read through it before we go, to make sure they understand what I've written. They appreciate that my kids are easy to look after as a result. Could you get your husband to speak to them, stressing the importance of the routine, and asking them to respect your wishes? It might be better coming from him.' **Laura**

'In my experience, dealing with in-laws requires a great deal of patience and humility. It's likely that your mother-in-law will have strong ideas about how children should be brought up, and that these will not always correspond with your decisions. When the children spend time with my in-laws, I allow myself to be flexible. I give my mother-in-law guidance as to what is normal for the children, but leave the ultimate decision up to her. I can't say it's not a shock to see my toddler sleeping soundly on the sofa at 11pm when we return from dinner, but so far it has done him no permanent damage, and has served to make our relationships run a little more smoothly!' **Kim**

'I agree with Kim. It is completely understandable that mums don't want their babies' routines upset, but some-times it's important to compromise. Perhaps the answer is to leave your son with your mother-in-law at a time when it is least likely to disturb his routine. But, it is important to show trust in your in-laws, for everyone's sake. It would be unfor-tunate to deny grandparents access to their grandchildren, simply because of fear of upsetting routines. Allowing the routine to drift may result in your baby being a little over-tired, but if this is the price for improved relationships all round, then it is probably worth it.' **Gill**

'Try to remember the positive things about grandparents: they have time and patience to focus on their grandchild, and they don't complain about having to read the same book 20 times in a row! And children recognise the special love that grandparents reserve entirely for them. It's so worth building and developing a working relationship with grandparents. Remember, play dates aren't just for kids – invite a granny along! Include lunch or coffee, and all have fun together, without it involving too much effort.' **Briony**

'Just a thought ... I hope we're all reading very carefully as, guess what, one day we'll all be mothers-in-law! I wonder what we'll be like. Flexible, understanding, non-judgemental, generous, open-minded ... I'm sure!' **Ruth**

'I am lucky with my in-laws, but do feel that I should be a better daughter-in-law. I have never given my baby to them for the day and have always been there at the same time. I think they have now given up asking to take him out. I suspect they see me as over-protective. I think it will always be different with daughters and their mums; my mum sees the baby every day and has him at least once a week. But we all need to keep making the effort with our in-laws for the sake of our children and our husbands.' **Nicola**

**Gina says:** My advice is to ask grandparents to respect your way of bringing up your children, and if they are not happy about what you are doing, to wait and discuss it with you once the children are out of earshot. Remember, conversation is a two-way thing, so listen to them as well. After all, they have been through all of this before as parents themselves. Be patient, and try to find ways you can meet each other halfway.

## ■ Mum-to-Mum: *Making comparisons with other mums*

### Query

*'My sister-in-law had a baby six months after me. Since then I have been comparing myself with her, and find myself feeling envious as she seems to have found it all so easy. When I tell her how hard I have found it, she says how it all comes naturally and being a mum is easier than working. Also, she has now gone back to work because my mother-in-law, who is retired, is looking after her baby for her. She hasn't shown as much interest in my daughter and my mum is not able to give the same support to me.'* **Fee**

### Answers

'Don't worry; I think everyone compares their parenting skills to another mother's at some time or another. My husband is in the forces, so we have moved every two years, and that means new friends and a new house every time, so I also found motherhood hard. Many times, I wished my mum or friends lived nearby, so I could pop in for a chat or some support. I understand your frustration at feeling left out, but try to keep your chin up. If something is really bothering you, do think about mentioning it – just choose the right time to raise it.' **Louise**

'This reminds me of how I felt with certain friends. I met a lot of new people in my antenatal class. At the time it was great, as we were all expecting our first babies. Six months down the line, however, I realised that a few of my 'new friends' were not making me feel good about myself. Suddenly I found that having a baby was a competitive sport, and I have always been rubbish at sport. Perfect Matilda was sleeping through the night at two weeks, while Wonderful William was speaking at six months, and so it went on. I used to come home from seeing them thinking that I was doing something wrong and that my perfectly normal three-month-old was developmentally behind. After a stern talking-to by my husband, I thought about my new friends and realised that, if it wasn't for babies, we wouldn't have much in common. I suddenly felt empowered enough to edit the competitive women from my life and only see the ones that I felt easy with. No longer did we sit and talk about how wonderful everything was, but we talked about our "real" lives. Obviously it's a bit different with a family member, but just accept that she may not be the best person to share your experiences with, and keep your personal concerns for your more sympathetic friends.' **Judi**

'My relationship with my own mother is so much more important to me than that with my mother-in-law. So it follows that the same may be true for your mother-in-law's relationship with her daughter. The situation is probably more normal than you think – and your in-laws probably don't deliberately set out to exclude you; maybe they just don't think. The only advice I can give is to accept that your family is yours and your husband's is his, but they are all your daughter's family and she will probably love them all to bits.' **Ruth**

**Gina says:** Every mother's parenting experience is different and you are undoubtedly doing better than you think. Try to focus on what you have achieved, not what you haven't. Congratulate yourself on the fact that you have managed with much less help than your sister-in-law – this is a big achievement in itself. And, remember, you don't really know your sister-in-law's true situation, only the parts she wants you to know. Remember, no one is the perfect mother or has the perfect baby. They simply do not exist!

## Looking after your relationship

Time for you as a couple is not a luxury – it is a necessity. Of course life is challenging when faced with a change; however, it need not be a treadmill. If you have support with childcare, use it. If not, consider safeguarding specific times such as an hour or two, a couple of evenings a week, when the computers are off, the phones are off or unplugged and you can both settle down for a cuddle and a catch-up. You need to be mindful of the distinction between you being parents and partners – there is a place for each role, but you need to ensure that the couple who first made the decision to start the family are nurtured as well.

## Date night

Going out with your husband alone in the evening is often the last thing you think you want – however, it is often exactly the thing you need. CLB mum Judi says, 'It is so easy to live in a bubble when a baby comes along. After six months, you'll suddenly realise that you have not been alone with your partner, except in bed, and you may find it difficult to remember the last time you had a non-baby-related conversation.' Mum Laura says, 'Make a "date" with your partner, even if you don't go out. I know it's corny and clichéd, but how else do you make time for each other when there are so many other things to think about?' Something simple such as going out once a fortnight to a local restaurant to share a pizza and a bottle of wine may not be an earth-shattering move, but it can have a profound effect on your relationship.

### Mums' Top Tips

❀ 'On Saturday afternoons when our baby's napping, we love to go back to bed for a cuddle. It feels really special and almost naughty! If it's a lovely day, we go and sit in the garden with a glass of wine. It's tempting to start doing something useful, but we reckon that our relationship is more important than housework!' **Marie**

✿ 'Try to stick to your planned dates. Even if you set a date in your mind, it's all too easy to find excuses when the time comes, so block-book the babysitter for the next three months. Then, unless it is an emergency, do not cancel. You may not always feel like going on this date, but you'll be surprised that no matter how tired you are, putting on a touch of lipstick and sitting in a local restaurant for a couple of hours makes you feel part of normal life again; it also focuses back on the two of you as a couple.' **Judi**

## Disagreements

You and your partner will both want the best for your children, but it is normal to sometimes disagree on how to go about this. At these times, try not to simply be stubborn; force yourself to take a step back and try to be open-minded. Think 'Would I rather be right or happy?' and pick your battles carefully. When you do disagree, try not to argue in front of your baby, however young she is, as she is likely to pick up on the tension. It's better to just leave the room, or walk around the block, until you feel calm again and then discuss it later when you are alone together.

Keep talking to one another. Good communication lies at the heart of tackling difficulties and, if you can talk openly and listen well, then any issue can be dealt with. There may be times when you really are struggling to communicate. At these times try speaking to a friend you can trust. Just talking about something can help enormously. Also, it's surprising how often friends will tell you that they have felt exactly the same way about their partner. I have sometimes been astonished at the stories from couples who I thought never argued. So, don't feel as though you are the only one having problems. In my experience, you won't need to look far to find a sympathetic ear.

Babies are expensive and one of the main causes of disagreements between new parents is financial difficulties. It's easy to bury your head in the sand and try to believe that you will manage somehow but the pressures will soon start to build and you will become resentful when your partner spends money on things you don't consider necessary. Rather than arguing, sit down and look at the figures properly. List your priorities and where you can realistically make savings. Then set up a joint account for all the essential bills and a small private account each. That way if and when you want to treat yourself to something extra, you can easily work out if you can afford it. It takes a little bit of time to organise this, but it is worth the effort. It will mean that your financial situation is more under control and no longer such a worry and this will benefit your relationship.

## Mums' Top Tips

❀ 'Remember to show your appreciation for what the other does. Caring for a baby is tough, but so is going to work and worrying about supporting a growing family's needs. I know my husband loves it when I tell him that he is doing a good job, and he in turn praises me. Everyone likes to be recognised for what they are contributing – and praise and thanks cost nothing!' **Gill**

❀ 'Sometimes when my husband and I disagree, listening becomes more difficult and it is easy for misunderstand-ings to develop into full-blown arguments. When this happens, I just walk away. It annoys my husband, who prefers arguing, but even he understands that it gets us nowhere. Because we now recognise this pattern, we can often laugh about it before the situation deteriorates.' **Angela**

❀ 'Now for one of my most-hated management phrases – "Make sure you are singing from the same hymn sheet." In fact, running the house is not dissimilar to being a manager at work. I make sure everyone involved in my children's care is informed and in agreement with the way things are done. Sometimes, my husband and I even have the equivalent of team meetings!' **May**

❧ 'My kids both go to nursery one day a week, and that's my day off. It means I don't feel bitter about being the "primary carer" the other six days. But my husband has a stressful job and he needs a break too. At the moment, he doesn't get any time off as he's home the kids want to be round him. I think it's important that time off is shared as well as the work, so we are addressing this and trying to create some gaps for both of us.' **Laura**

## ■ Mum-to-Mum: *Relationship difficulties*

### Query

*'Since having children, my husband and I are finding it harder to make things work between us. We seem to bicker and argue all the time, and weekends are a nightmare. Yesterday, I was so close to asking him to move out. I know we have stopped trying to make time for each other. Also, he tries to help out, but it's almost easier without him. Recently he was away for a week, and I found it nice to have a break. The house and kids ran like clockwork, and I didn't have any expectations that could then be shattered. Our marriage is at an all-time low and I feel sad and confused. When do you call it a day? How do you know if it's still worth fighting for? I love him, but it's falling apart.'* **Fee**

### Answers

'I think, as mums, we need to make time for "us" on a regular basis, so we have a chance to remember that we were individuals and part of a couple, before ultimately becoming a family. My New Year's resolution is to make time for my husband and to get out together alone. We need this to balance the family time. Don't be too hasty with any decisions. Try to create some quality time as a couple, and see where things go from there.' **Sarah**

'If you are close to your family, could you and the children go and visit for a while? This might give you some time on your own and a chance to chat things through with your mum. Plus, your husband can then see how much he misses all of you. Having a baby definitely disrupts and changes everything. I don't know any friends who haven't struggled through rough spots in their marriages once children arrive; you are not alone. Would your husband go to marriage counselling? It's bound to be a bumpy road, but counselling could help to get you communicating again.' **Rebecca**

'I think a heart-to-heart would be a good way forward. I don't know what your husband is like, but I know that my husband tells me he feels left out and "functional" when all my attention is on the baby. He quite often talks to me and I zone out, as I'm too focused on her. This leaves him feeling a bit like "excess baggage" and uncared for. I am not in any way blaming you, but do you think this might be part of the problem?' **Emma**

'We all have our moments of irritation; you just have to persevere. That is partly what marriage is all about. Some phases are better than others and we have to communicate and trust one another to get through the hard times. If you still love your husband, then there is hope. If you don't care at all, then you have to worry! Have you spoken to him about your feelings? I once lost the plot with my husband about him not helping around the house, and he replied that he had no idea that I was suffering. After that, he proceeded to help, and all I had to do was ask. So, try talking … it helps.' **Amy**

'Do either of you have any male friends or relatives that have children, who could then talk to your husband? He needs to understand how difficult your role is and how hard you're working to create a happy family home. He might just need a friendly and unbiased third party to help him understand your needs better.' **Gerry**

'At present, you are in a circle of stress and fear, but it will get better. Maybe you could ask your relatives or a friend to help. Most of us don't feel comfortable asking, but when you are feeling so down, sometimes you have to step outside your comfort zone and trust the help of others.' **Daisy**

'You are both going through a difficult time at the moment; raising two young children is enjoyable, but also so demanding. Some men rebel: they see their partners spending all their time and emotional energy on the children. You don't have the inclination to spoil him as you used to, and he may see this as rejection. I am sure he still loves you, but he doesn't get to see "you" much, and needs reminding of who "you" are. The main thing is, you have both changed over the last few years and you both need to learn to adapt to this change. If you don't spend enough quality time together, it's easy to forget why you love one another. Try to spend some time together, even if it's just a short night out. Forget about being parents, and remind each other of your qualities as individuals. Only you know for sure, but it seems as if your marriage is worth fighting for.' **Louise**

'You are definitely not alone. We have just had the worst weekend ever. We've got two gorgeous girls, but only 14 months apart, and we are constantly competing to see who is the most tired. I know this sounds childish, but I guess exhaustion does strange things to us all. It's sad, as we used to have so much fun together, and now all we seem to do is bicker. You're right; although the week is busy, it seems to run smoother without him around. I've decided today, however, that I'm going to "find myself" again by getting fit and taking up an evening class. I'm sure that by rediscovering myself as a person, I'll be able to cope better and be more tolerant of my husband. I will also have something else to talk about, other than nappies and feeds!' *Sarah*

'It sounds like you and your husband are on the same side, but it's easy to think that you're not when the pressure's on. One absolute luxury for Dan and me has been to go away without the children; even if it's just for one night. Both of us always come back feeling 10 years younger. If you can't do that, make your evenings together really special. Candles, wine, soft music and some nice lingerie do it for us!' **Leisa**

'Keep talking. I don't think men pick up on things the way women do. I often get comments like, "Why didn't you ask?" or, "Why didn't you tell me?" I think, "Why should I have to?", but men sometimes need things spelled out. Now, he does the laundry and I do the folding; he cleans the kitchen and I do the cooking. It really helps and I also let him know how much I appreciate it.' **Cathy**

'It's all about compromise. You probably *will* argue in the beginning – sleep deprivation and the responsibility of a tiny baby do not always make for a good mood – but it is how you choose to behave afterwards that counts. When you've both calmed down, talk about things and reach a compromise that you both agree with and which seems fair. Having a baby is hard work, but once you've got things worked out, it's a lot more relaxing.' **Debbie**

**Gina says:** Fee received some invaluable advice from the CLB mums. One piece that stood out for me was from

Caroline. She said she realised that she and her husband needed to get to know the new 'us'; the mum and the dad, rather than start waiting for each other to act as they did before they had kids. She had to make a real effort to break the cycle of feeling resentful and irritable. Easier said than done, but it was worth it. She also had to get her husband to understand that relationships are a two-way thing and maybe he needed to give her more of a chance to get back on top. You'll be pleased to know that Fee did work things out! She says: 'Thank you everyone for your valuable advice and support. I am now making more time for myself, and we are trying to make time for each other again. So, if anyone else feels like I did, don't be too hard on yourself. Try to step back and look at the bigger picture; speak to your partner openly and honestly; try going with your instincts more, and forget about mess; life's too short. The main thing is to try to find a way to enjoy things – even if it is just one thing a day, one day at a time.'

## Getting your partner involved

At first, your baby will demand so much of your time, especially if you are breastfeeding, that sometimes your partner may feel left out and almost jealous. It is important to get him more involved. He may not do things exactly the same way as you, but try to sit on your hands and bite your tongue and not interfere too much. He may see interference as criticism and it will knock his confidence in caring for the baby. Your partner may not be as good as you at looking after your little one, but as long as your baby is secure and happy, let him get on with it and grab the valuable 'me-time' while you can.

Be careful not to involve your partner only when you are at the end of your tether, or when your baby is crying. If he enjoys the time he spends with the baby, he is more likely to seek more of it. Of course, that doesn't mean *don't* involve him to help out when your baby is irritable, but don't *only* involve him in those situations. The time you might most want help is when you've been only with your baby all day and are desperate for a break. But try not to thrust the baby into your partner's arms the minute he walks in the door. It may be tempting, as you will literally have been counting the minutes until he gets home, but if he has 15 minutes to unwind and get changed, he will be far more willing to muck in.

### Mums' Top Tips

🌸 'I like the way men take a different approach. My husband is far more hands-on with the kids than I am. He includes them in what he's doing and can make the most boring job a fun thing. I think it's really important to recognise that there are different approaches and they all have their merits.' **Gem**

❀ 'When our son was born, my husband held him and
dressed him for the first time. He said this made him feel
proud, as he wouldn't have thought himself capable. At
home, I would ask if he wanted to change or bath him,
and just stayed near enough to guide him through the
process, without dampening his efforts. Within days my
husband had turned into a confident father. I also express
milk, so my husband can feed our baby and bond with
him too. On Sunday mornings they have father-and-son
time; my husband does breakfast and gets the baby
ready for the day, while I have a lie-in. I feel that, because
my husband is so hands-on, either of us can care for our
baby and I don't feel solely responsible.' **Kelly**

❀ 'There are some things Daddy just does better, such
as rough play! I love watching my partner playing with
our little one during bathtime or changing time.
Because I do it more often, it is seen as a task but
when he does it, it's a game and our baby giggles and
laughs all the time.' **Emma**

❀ 'At first, we had the routine typed up and on the fridge
so my partner knew what the baby needed and when. It
made him feel more confident as a dad, and also more
involved. Of course, he felt the need to tell me in detail
what he had done and I would have to say well done;
but so what, he *had* done well! In the process, I get a

couple of hours off and, much as I love my baby and miss him like crazy, it is also nice to have a break without worrying.' **Debbie**

❀ 'I find the best way to get my partner involved is to give him *very* specific instructions. It's no good assuming that he will change the baby's T-shirt if it is soaking wet or tidy away the highchair; so I now leave very clear instructions about what I expect to happen when I'm not there. He may not like the instructions, but I find it's the only way to get him to do more than the bare minimum.' **Kim**

❀ 'I used to yell at my husband for things I'm now relaxed about. All I'm really interested in is the safety and happiness of my child. So, if you want your husband involved, try to be supportive and gentle. Men like to think they know best and can get defensive when they realise they don't!' **Laura**

❀ 'Men don't think about all the things we have to do. I decided to write a list of all the chores I had to get done on a daily, weekly and monthly basis. When we were both relaxing after the kids had gone to bed, I produced my list and asked him to make his. My partner responded, rather shamefully, that he didn't have enough things to put on a list. It really helps men to realise that you need their support and, in the process, you'll amaze yourself with how much you do – so feel proud!' **Gem**

✿ 'I need to be more forthcoming about asking my husband to do things with our toddler. I tend to take over, because it comes more naturally to me. Today I specifically asked my husband to do breakfast and he really enjoyed it. It's a bit frustrating having to ask and be "thankful" when they do something, but I guess positive reinforcement is all part of the training!' **Rebecca**

✿ 'If you want your husband to help you more, talking is a must. Always start with the positive bits first. Tell him that what he did was great, but if he did this too, it might help. Don't tell him he did something wrong; instead, discuss things in a non-blaming way!' **Amanda**

## ▮ Mum-to-Mum: *Sharing the care*

### Query

*Last night my husband and I both woke up with stomach pains and vomiting, and we concluded that it must be food poisoning. Neither of us got any more sleep and, as our baby is teething at the moment, he woke three times between 5am and 7am. Both of us feel terrible and can barely keep fluids down, so tell me this – why am I the one who's got up with our baby, while my husband's still asleep in bed?'* **Gem**

## Answers

'We should be equal to men on all levels, but I think it's unachievable. What bothers me, however, is that what I call "parenting", my partner calls "babysitting". He does his bit, so I can have time off, but he thinks I should be thankful, rather than seeing it as his responsibility.' **Laura**

'Perhaps you need to sit down with your husband and explain to him that you really need his support. Childcare is a joint responsibility.' **Kasia**

**Gina says:** This is a common problem faced by couples, along with the general argument about who does the most/who's the most tired. I liked Izzie's approach. She says: 'This is just a legacy from the old days, when childcare was seen as a woman's responsibility. This attitude can only be changed by women, and we should seek to do it in clever ways, without causing too much conflict. I bet the majority of mums are still facing this problem, but we should not simply accept it. We need to work on training our husbands! One thing we can do for the next generation is to teach our sons about sharing responsibility in the house, and to encourage them to help with the housework. In this way, they are more likely to be supportive in a future relationship, and have a happier family life as a result.'

# Your sex life ... what sex life?!

In the months after the arrival of your baby, you might hate the thought of having sex. You will be sore, tired and no doubt have the libido of a dying fly! What can help, though, is to maintain some physical closeness, such as kissing, cuddling and holding hands when you go out for a walk. Tell your partner how you are feeling as this can make you feel more relaxed about everything. Eventually, when you feel ready, gradually become more intimate by giving each other gentle massages and skin-to-skin cuddles; your sex life will slowly return. If you have had stitches or are worried about pain, think about using gentle caresses or oral sex to bring each other to orgasm, rather than trying penetration. By being patient and talking to one another, any blip will only be temporary.

Many couples wonder when it is safe to start having sex again after the birth of their baby. There aren't any hard-and-fast rules about this: traditional advice used to be to wait until your postnatal check-up at six weeks after the birth, but you may find you're ready much earlier, or later. One school of thought says it's better to have sex before your check-up so that, if you do experience pain or other problems, you can discuss it with your GP at the time of the examination.

To have sexual relations, you obviously need to spend time together! Arrange a babysitter and go out for the evening, or have a candlelit dinner at home, to remind yourselves that you were lovers first before you were parents. Also, if you do have concerns about your sex life, it can be easier to talk things through away from home.

## Physical discomfort

You may find sex painful in the first few weeks after the birth if your perineum is still bruised from stitches or tears. You may also find your caesarean scar is sore for a few weeks until it has properly healed; so, if this is the case, wait until it feels more comfortable. Likewise, you may experience vaginal discharge for several weeks after the birth, and this may put you off sex too.

To help restore pelvic tone after a vaginal birth, try practising pelvic-floor exercises – gently squeeze your muscles, as if you're holding in wind, tense for a few seconds and then release. Pilates exercises are also good for improving pelvic strength. After having a C-section, Debbie found man-on-top positions uncomfortable. She said, 'See it as an opportunity to try new positions – it may even spice up your sex life! It did take a while before we found out what suited us but we had fun trying!'

If you are breastfeeding, try feeding your baby before you have sex to minimise the risk of leaking milk at an intimate moment. You can always wear breast pads if it makes you feel better – and just try to laugh about it with your partner! And be aware of the myth that you can't get pregnant if you're breastfeeding – because you can! If you are fully breastfeeding, this does give a high degree of protection against getting pregnant, but there are no guarantees. Beware of the dangers of the weeks when you are trying to phase out breastfeeding, as you will ovulate before your period arrives. Periods usually return after six to ten weeks if you're bottle-feeding or combining breast-feeding with bottles.

## Mums' Top Tips

❀ 'I found the fact that I was breastfeeding made a huge difference when we started doing "it" after our baby was born. I was much drier down below than I was before having her, and my GP said this was totally normal and to get some lubricant (water-based if you're using condoms). It really helped. It was still sore though; it took a few months to feel okay. I found I needed lots more foreplay than before (and a couple of glasses of wine) to help me relax but, even then, it wasn't exactly 100 per cent comfortable for ages. I was also told that an oestrogen cream can soothe the dryness.' **Laura**

❀ 'There's a saying that goes, "Love is a muscle; it must be exercised, or it can become weak." This really helps me to focus. It takes effort to feel sexy (so that you want someone to think that you are desirable); it takes effort to wear

nice clothes and put on perfume; it takes effort to give
your partner a cuddle; it takes effort to just concentrate on
loving by giving.' **Michelle**

❀ 'I'm ready for bed by 10pm, but my husband is a night
owl. So once dinner was over, I would head upstairs for a
shower, then put on some sexy undies and high heels and
go and get my hubby! He thinks it's fab, and his reaction
in turn makes me feel more confident about my post-
pregnancy body. It also means that I am in bed by 10pm!
Audrey Hepburn said, "The less you make love, the less
you will feel like making love." It's all in the mind for a
woman, so start thinking of yourself as a sexy woman!
I bet you are anyway!' **Jo**

❀ 'I think sex should be scheduled into your routine! I am
shattered by the end of the day and find mornings a much
better time! But whatever works for you … Once you get
back into it, it's cool.' **Fee**

❀ 'I finally achieved my pre-baby weight just before my son's
first birthday (my long-term, realistic target) and, with a
great haircut two weeks ago, I am just beginning to feel
good about myself again. I had a forceps delivery and a
very nasty tear. I was really worried that things would
have changed forever, but I am pleased to report that it
does get better. A few of my friends have had weekends

away with their hubbies *sans* baby. My friends have said that having time alone together really helped them to rediscover the special something in their relationships and that they owed the time to their husbands. Worth considering.' **Janie**

## Emotional issues

Emotionally, you may still be too wrapped up in looking after your baby to think about sex. Just remember, all of these thoughts are normal. Whatever your reasons for not wanting sex, don't forget to describe (tactfully) how you're feeling to your partner. Explain that your feelings are temporary and that you still love him. Try to show him affection, as this is the classic time for him to feel rejected. Be creative about other ways of finding intimacy together; for example, kissing and stroking. Penetrative sex is not the only way of showing your love for one another.

## Seeking help

If you are finding it difficult to resolve problems with your sex life, consider attending therapy, such as that provided by Relate, the marriage guidance charity. You will discuss your difficulties and what you want to change and then be given a programme of exercises designed to increase the intimacy between you. You may feel embarrassed at first but it will be worth this to have your full loving relationship back. Talking to a sympathetic and knowledgeable third party may actually save your relationship. For more information, log on to www.relate.org.uk.

**CLB Mums' Top 10 Best Ways ... to
Revive Your Sex Life**

1. Understand that sex after birth is different for different people. Some people are back on form in two weeks, yet for the majority, it takes much longer. Don't leave it too long. I personally felt that by six months I needed to get moving. I think it's normal to worry about how it will be (especially for those who have had stitches), but eventually you just have to get on with it – and you'll probably surprise yourself!

2. Follow a routine for your child that has them in bed at 7pm! There's nothing more off-putting than the exhaustion of caring for a young baby, but if you and your husband are able to enjoy some time together in the evening, then you are much more likely to connect on an intimate level.

3. Most times we need to connect with our partners on a mental level, before we can connect with them in a physical way. Talking openly about your feelings and having fun together is the best tonic for maintaining a good sex life.

4. Recognise that your partner has urges that you will never replicate. So, sometimes you may just have to grin and bear it!

5. If you aren't ready to have sex, go easy on your partner. Tread carefully and be sensitive when you are saying no. It is very demoralising to be physically rejected by the person you love.

6. If sex is uncomfortable, try new positions. It took us a while to find what suited us, but I'd say the baby's arrival has actually spiced up our sex life!

7. Try not to tense up at the thought that it might hurt – lots of foreplay and wine helps!

8. Organise a 'date night'. On our date night we would order takeaway, express the baby's feed then drink a bottle of wine. The rest just kind of follows.

9. We always make an effort to have frequent kisses and cuddles, and we always kiss goodbye and kiss goodnight. Closeness is not just about sex and, as long as you continue to be open and emotionally close, the sexual side of things will come back.

10. Pamper yourself and spend time on your appearance. If you feel good about yourself, you're more likely to want to get physical with your partner.

## ■ Mum-to-Mum: *No desire for sex*

### Query

*'During my pregnancy and since the arrival of our baby (he's now four months old), I have had absolutely no desire for sex. It is now over a year since we last had sex and I don't know what to do. It is like that part of my body has shut down. I am worried about the long-term effect this is having on our relationship. I still love my husband and find him attractive, but I don't feel good about myself any more. All I see when I look in the mirror is stretch marks and flabby bits. I am also terrified that sex is going to hurt. Has anyone been through this, or is it just me?'* **Rachael**

### Answers

'Not having the desire for sex is totally normal. I experienced this after the arrival of each of my children, and between one pregnancy and the next. I love my husband dearly, and he is understanding and patient, but I believe sex is an important part of a couple's life, and it is important to get the desire back somehow. The thought of sex can be worse than the action. A bit like going to the gym – you can't be bothered to go, but once you are there, you enjoy it and feel better after. I wish that there was a magic pill to take, but I think we have to remember what our bodies have gone through with pregnancy, birth, breastfeeding and sleepless nights. Is it any surprise that we aren't in the mood?' **Nicola**

'I know you must feel like your baby's been around forever, but four months is nothing at all. Your hormones are still settling down, and your body, thanks to Mother Nature, is saying a firm 'No' to any possibility of getting pregnant again this early. So it's really not your fault that you don't feel like sex! On top of this, you've had a huge physical demand from pregnancy and birth, you will be tired and you will still be adjusting mentally to your new responsibilities, so realistically, sex is not going to be top of your list! I would try to talk to your husband about this, if you haven't already.' **Sharon**

'I'm afraid I'm one of those "back in the saddle quickly" girls: two weeks! I'm not saying this to make you feel inadequate, but to encourage you. Often these days, my husband will make amorous advances, and I'm not feeling like it at all. However, he's very gentle and persistent, and usually has me gearing up within minutes! Anyhow, my point is that I think it's his gentle understanding and persuasion that gets me every time. My advice would be to sit down with your husband and explain that you understand how he feels, and that you would like to resume things again, but that it's imperative he is patient with you. If you take one small step to heal things, he will appreciate this and be more inclined to be patient.' **Kim**

A while ago I was in exactly the same situation with regard to not wanting sex. I just wasn't interested and would quite happily have never done it again. But that wasn't fair on my hubby and, when we did it, I really enjoyed it. I couldn't understand why I had been so reluctant. It is now getting easier and more regular; still less than once a month, but it was only once every six months before, so there is improvement – and hope!' **Felicity**

'Am I the only one *not* being pestered for sex?! Seriously, I thought I would give you a view from the other side, as in our house it is my husband who can't be bothered with sex – and me who would be at it like a rabbit, given half a chance! But four months isn't that long so, as others have said, give yourself time.' **Stacey**

**Gina says:** I agree with the mums that patience and communication are key. Even the happiest marriages can take a knock in the bedroom after the arrival of a baby. But avoiding the subject of sex is the worst thing you can do. Instead, share your worries with your partner. This will help manage expectations and relieve any pressure to get back in the saddle before you're both ready. Arm yourself with post-birth essentials, such as lubricant and massage oil, and take things slowly. Keep talking, flirting and cuddling, but sex can take up to a year to get back on track. The most important thing is that you remain intimate and close until it does.

# Keeping in touch with old friends

Don't neglect your friends. There will come a time, when you've got through the early months, that you will have more time for them. If you haven't made the effort to stay in contact, they may have moved on and left you behind. At first they will be all over you and your baby, but they will soon get bored with endless tales of poo and possetting! Invite them over for dinner or just a drink after your little one has gone to bed. It's a way of still seeing them, without having the hassle of carting heaps of baby gear with you.

You will, inevitably, grow apart from some friends as your circumstances change, but you will make more. Antenatal classes, baby and toddler groups and baby classes are a great way to get out and meet other parents in your area. Having the same responsibilities as you, they will understand why you are 20 minutes late, and won't moan because your baby was sick all over you just as you were about to leave!

## Mums' Top Tips

❧ 'Make an effort to have child-free outings with your friends, especially the ones who don't have kids themselves. It makes it easier to have an adult conversation. I've found it quite hard to keep up the friendship with my oldest friend, who doesn't have kids, but making time for her is important – as is recognising that she's not as interested in my children as I am!' **Laura**

✿ 'Since it's now more difficult for us to go out, we have friends without kids round to us for a takeaway. This way, we still get to catch up. We also make an effort to meet up for a meal or cinema visit every six weeks and we keep in touch weekly, even if it's just a text to say hello. Try to find that old common ground, rather than talking about babies all night.' **Kelly**

✿ 'I can see how becoming a mother is a completely over-whelming experience, and it is difficult to get off the subject. But I can also see it from the "child-free" side. I, therefore, try to be patient with my friends who don't have children and make an effort not to talk about my baby for as long as I can – not often that long!' **Mel**

✿ 'It's challenging to keep in touch with old friends after you have children because your life invariably moves in differ-ent directions. I also found, as a stay-at-home mum, that I didn't have much else to talk about. The way around it for me is to try to catch up with old friends once every couple of months. That way you'll have loads of chat saved up that doesn't involve babies! I also find it helps to get together in a group.' **Kim**

❀ 'I spend lots of time emailing my friends. We are all so busy, either with kids or work, and email gives us the chance to chat at a time to suit. One of my old friends has no kids and a busy career, but we try and see each other occasionally and email all the time. Another friend is single, but I see lots of her as she loves the children, and likes to come and give me a hand.' **Claire**

## ◼ Mum-to-Mum: *Family conflict*

### Query

*'My brother-in-law is getting married in Brazil in December and is expecting us all to go to his wedding. My husband has recently broached the subject with him of us not being able to afford to go, together with the childcare diffi-culties, yet my brother-in-law has taken it badly and is very hurt that we are not planning to come. My husband is now thinking of taking out a loan to pay for it. I understand why my brother-in-law might be disappointed, but I just wish he understood how hard it can be when you have young children. Am I being unreasonable?'* **May**

### Answer

'Don't go! Even if you could afford it, why would you want the hassle? I know people travel long-haul with very young kids and survive, but it is not ideal.' **Laura**

'I certainly wouldn't take out a loan to pay for such a trip; it isn't fair on you, and it will be another burden that you don't need. Priorities do change with the arrival of kids, and friends and family who understand this are the ones that count.' **Avrilf**

'I really wouldn't go to Brazil in your circumstances. I think your brother-in-law is being rather selfish. I get cross when people arrange overseas weddings and then get distraught when people say they can't go. Not everyone can just hop on a plane at the drop of a hat! So, don't feel guilty. Just say sorry, but stick to your guns.' **Kay**

'I feel that the situation calls for a compromise and that your husband should go alone. I know that money's important, but so is family.' **Carole**

'I think it is important for your husband to go to his brother's wedding. However, as money is an issue, I would suggest he has a discreet word with his parents, explaining your current financial pressures. Perhaps the family could then lend you some cash, rather than paying credit card companies' insane rates of interest.' **Ellie**

'We got married in New York. If people could come, we were delighted, but if not, there was no resentment towards anyone. Many family members couldn't make it, so we had a second celebration in the UK at later date. Would your brother-in-law consider this option? It may suit other family members too.' **Amanda**

**Gina says:** This is a tricky one. CLB mum Bridget's advice was great – she said, 'My suggestion would be to arrange for the whole thing to be recorded on DVD and for you to pay for it as a gift. That way you would get to see it and still be involved.'

## Summary – points to remember

- To enhance any relationship, keep communicating.

- Good relationships are all about compromise, so be prepared to listen and find the middle ground.

- Grandparents may have different views on childcare from you, but they also have a lifetime of experience, so try to be objective.

- Let minor criticisms wash over you and trust your own instincts and decision-making.

- If there has been a disagreement with loved ones, find a good moment to talk about things rationally. Discussing things when everyone is heated will often make things worse.

- Re-establishing a good sex life can be a gradual process. Cuddle and caress, even if you don't feel like making love. And talk to each other about how you are feeling. You'll enjoy intimacy again when the time is right.

- If you fall out, agree to take it in turns to explain how you feel. Be honest, listen and try not to blame each other. Focus on reaching a compromise, rather than proving your point – and don't bring up past resentments, which will get in the way of resolving the current situation.

- Help to involve your partner in hands-on childcare. Encourage him without being critical, and don't worry if he does things differently. It's in everyone's interest to share the load.

- Don't assume that your partner can guess what you want – always tell him.

- Make a date with your partner, share some quality time as a couple and try to make each other feel loved.

- Remember to make time for old friends. Find new ways to meet up that suit you all, and try not to talk babies all night.

# 4

# Mums on the Move

From a first stroll to the park with a new baby to flying to the Caribbean or hiking up a Scottish Munro, the parents who've contributed to this book have been there and done it. Their knowledge and experience will supply you with invaluable advice for planning any kind of trip, straight from the horse's mouth. In the early days, just getting out of the house can be a challenge. However, it's so important for both you and your baby to get out in the fresh air, to meet friends or visit places that are stimulating and fun. Getting out and about is important for your wellbeing, especially if prior to having your baby you enjoyed an active social life. Seeing friends and family can be a lifeline in the early days when you are making that challenging adjustment to motherhood.

CLB mum Emma really hits the spot when she says: 'Make the effort … It can be easy not to and sometimes to use the routines as an excuse not to get out, but the routines are flexible enough.' Many mums made the point that outings were easier if you always had a bag packed and ready to go by the door or in the car: it's a good habit to get into.

Another worry is going to a new place where you think a child will be expected to keep quiet – for example, a church service. In this section, you'll find both reassurance and good advice about this challenging outing.

One mum's anxiety about a long car journey prompted supportive comments and some great ideas. Two of them stood out: frequent stops on the way and making sure you've got the right tapes or CDs to keep your little ones both soothed and distracted.

All the parents who've been able to afford the time and money to go on holiday seem to concur with CLB mum Karen's comment: 'Obviously packing is a great big faff and the flight can be a bit testing, but it's absolutely worth it.' And there can be some refreshing surprises when you go abroad. Janie found child-friendly Europe a welcome change from the rather grumpy UK: 'The great thing was that the attitude towards babies is so different in continental Europe; when we walked into a lovely restaurant with our baby in his buggy, diners actually smiled at us!'

Many parents with young babies necessarily leave little to chance when planning their break, and anticipating potential problems – both practically and mentally – will leave you able to cope if need be. Unless you're able to go to a hotel or resort that's fully set up for children – for example, going on a Neilson or Mark Warner holiday – it's maybe more relax-ing to take the self-catering option. 'Relaxing' might seem an odd thing to say, as of course you're not getting away from the cooking and washing-up, but worrying whether a hotel will warm a bottle at 2am or feeling embarrassed about your baby's antics in a highchair can seriously mar your holiday! You'll also find a host of sensible ideas of what to take, from having a packing list you can update on your computer to taking disposable bibs and pre-sterilised bottles.

When it comes to feeding on holiday, the CLB mums' main concerns are to do with keeping to routines and being able to buy the right sort of formula – or the right bottled water to make up formula – or baby food. The mums who've contributed tips to this book vary from the super-prepared holidaymaker who takes all her little one's favourite foods, to those who simply drop into the supermarket on the way to their holiday accommodation. There are some innovative companies recommended by parents, such as So Baby and Tiny Tots Away (see page 201), which will either prepare baby food for you to take with you or deliver baby necessities to your holiday address.

Holiday health concerns for babies tend to centre on sun and insect bites. The concerns many parents have about plane travel can often be neatly summed up as 'Is the pain worth the gain?'. You may think that a long journey in a confined space with limited entertainment, and then the adjustment to a new time zone, may just not be worth it. But as you will see from the tips supplied by CLB readers, taking a break abroad *is* worth the hassle, and with their help you will be prepared.

Perhaps the point to stress here is to check all the rules with the airline first, especially concerning baby food and milk in hand luggage, as they vary between airlines and change frequently. If you're relying on your child sitting in his own car seat on the plane, or you're desperate to take a breastfeeding pillow, or a pot of bubbles to amuse your little one on board, check what's allowed to avoid disappointment. Another good way to prepare is to steel yourself for delays and know you won't be able to watch the movie during the flight – that way you could end up being pleasantly surprised!

The CLB mums have also got some great tips to help your baby settle into new surroundings once you arrive at your destination.

While your baby is portable you can still enjoy hiking, and our mums have words of encouragement for those who want to make the most of the great outdoors. Camping, too, is fun with children of all ages, so read our essential nuggets of knowledge before you go.

Most of all, wherever you go, remember that you benefit from new surroundings and from getting away from the pressures of home and work. In addition, your little one will enjoy relaxed time with you and your partner, and a holiday doesn't mean that your routine will go to pot.

# Getting out of the house

Please don't fret if your baby's routine slips a little when you go out. I have always found that when a baby is contented, he is also adaptable, so enjoy days out. Some children are naturally sociable, while others find busy social activities overwhelming. If your baby or toddler seems exhausted after a busy day, make sure the following one is peaceful and predictable. Remember that a quiet day at home might seem boring to you, but it can be a great source of comfort to children who need routine with which to develop safely and at their own pace.

Make sure you get out to see friends every couple of days or so. You can fit your outings around the routines between 2pm and 5pm. Try to arrange a drive somewhere at lunchtime so your baby still gets his sleep. A walk in the park is a great way of getting back into shape and the fresh air will help your baby settle well at bedtime – 4pm is a good time to go out for this. Why not arrange to meet a friend and chat and walk at the same time?

Wherever you may be on your day out, do try to let your baby or toddler get some fresh air and exercise. If you are going to a friend's house or visiting family, it should still be possible for a baby to have a little kick on a blanket, or your toddler to have a run around. Fresh air often helps children to sleep better, so even if your child sleeps in the car, if he has had lots of fresh air and some exercise, he should still be shattered by bedtime. When out with a young baby, try to avoid passing him round too much, or he will end up being in someone's arms most of the time. I am sure family and friends will want a cuddle, but also explain how much your baby likes to stay on his mat and kick!

## Mums' Top Tips

❀ 'Keep a well-stocked changing bag by your front door and be sure to replenish its supplies after each outing. If you have an older baby or toddler, make sure the bag also contains some toys, a few non-perishable snacks (mini rice-cakes are ideal), a drinking cup, a few spoons, and a couple of bibs for unplanned meals out.' **Laura**

❀ 'I always have two baby bags packed with essentials as I'm not great at remembering to replenish the empty bag when I come home.' **Debbie**

❀ 'With three children we have to be super-organised, so we keep a fully stocked baby bag and a bag for the older two in the boot of the car. We always replenish what we use (nappies, clean clothes, etc.) after each trip out, then put the bag back into the car. This means we can just get into the car and go when need be. I keep a bottle of water, some dried fruit and rice cakes in there, too.' **Pippa**

❀ 'Try to walk as much as you can. It is good for you and for the children to get fresh air. My daughter has walked everywhere (i.e. not used the pushchair) since she was two-and-a-half years old.' **Claire**

❧ 'We can go out for lunch and our baby will fall asleep in the car on the way home; we then pop her into her cot afterwards.' **Emma**

❧ 'It took me three attempts to get on a bus with my buggy; I chickened out and went home the first two times! It can be very intimidating, especially in the middle of town. Other mums know there are limited spaces on a bus for buggies, so stand your ground: if you were there first, then get on first! Once on, make sure the buggy is secure and *put the brake on!* Sounds simple, but I forgot the first time and had to make a grab for a runaway buggy. Start getting yourself ready to go when you reach the stop before yours, as this way you will be prepared to get off and will feel less flustered. Choose quieter times to go on the bus if possible, and remember, the more you go out, the easier it gets. Practice makes perfect and a confident mum!' **Debbie**

## ■ Mum-to-Mum: *Disrupted routines*

### Query

*'My son is nine weeks old and is doing well on the six-to-eight-week routine. I have just been invited to a postnatal depression*

*group once a week, plus a coffee morning. I am worried about disrupting his routine, but I feel I really need to go to get some support. I just wondered what other people did with regards to outings and the disruptions they may cause. Both groups interfere with feed times or naps.'* **Dolly**

## Answers

'I think it's really important to get out of the house and see people to keep your sanity, although I know it's very hard in the early days and I didn't manage it very well! The more you try though, the easier it gets. A lot will depend upon how much you can get away with "tweaking" your little one's routines. Do give it a try; even if one day goes a bit wrong, it's usually back on track by the evening and you can try to tweak it in a different way the next time.' **Claire**

'If your sleep routine is well established, you might find that your little one drops off to sleep easily in the car seat or pushchair anyway. When this happens I usually transfer him to the cot when we get home, with a top-up of milk, or leave the baby to sleep in a dark corner of the room. I sometimes put him in his Grobag ready for his nap while we are still at playgroup so, if he's sleeping happily, I don't have to worry about removing outdoor clothing, etc. You're doing the right thing by getting out and socialising with other mums.' **Catriona**

'I've found it's best to "go with the flow" and not obsess if things don't run to time later on. If I know that lunch is going to be late then I "slip in" an extra bottle straight after the morning nap to keep my baby going that little bit longer. If she has 30 minutes' sleep when we're out, I just put her down for her nap that bit later.' **Kathryn**

**Gina says:** In general, and as I say in my book, *The New Contented Little Baby Book,* I do think it is important to stick to the routine as much as you can from day to day, but I do understand that it might be difficult when you have planned a day out. For short trips, such as a walk in the park or coffee with a friend, you can easily stick to the routine by simply arranging your outing around your baby's sleep time. Please note, however, that this does not work with very young babies, who usually fall asleep as soon as the pram starts moving. In the case of very young babies, I would suggest that an outing actually coincides with their sleep time, to avoid them sleeping for too long during the day. For advice on all aspects of your baby's routine, including how to adapt it in special circumstances, please refer to the book mentioned above.

# Special occasions

Think very carefully before accepting a wedding invitation with a new baby. I would recommend going only if it's a very, very close friend or relation. Never underestimate how exhausting you'll find it, or how exhausting the newborn will find it. Everyone will want to talk to you as a new mum and see the baby, but try to avoid playing 'pass the baby'.

Older babies are more complicated, as they want to be on the move, and the novelty of bending down to pull your toddler away from yet another handbag or glass of champagne soon wears off! And to complicate matters, the timings of weddings rarely work for babies or toddlers. My other tips are: remove any child from the church the moment he squeaks (some people are relaxed about this, but not all); and be prepared to go and sit away from the party in a quiet room to feed. Don't just assume it's okay to breast-feed openly in the church or at the reception. Your children are your responsibility – this may sound obvious, but it's worth remembering. It's difficult to be fully engaged at a social function while childminding small children!

If you want to take your child to regular church services, maybe go along without your baby the first time to find out if it's child-friendly. Most churches have family services on Sundays.

## Mums' Top Tips

❀ 'Sit behind people who have other kids, especially older ones, as they often "entertain" your little one for you. We try to find a row towards the back where we can block off the exits by one of us sitting at each end. Then the little one can wander a bit and you can make a quick exit if need be. Churches are usually quite used to children in services and most will have a crèche you can go to for at least part of the service.' **Helen**

❀ 'When my child is at church, I use crayons and paper for entertainment. Raisins are good as I put them in a small pot so it takes my daughter a while to finish the entire pot and occupies her in the process. Don't take breadsticks – too much mess!' **Rose**

❀ 'Most churches nowadays are much more accepting of babies and toddlers making noise; it's just part of life and I'm sure yours won't be the only one. My grandad is a vicar and he often says that it's lovely to hear kids in the congregation, as it's an indicator that future generations will still attend church. He just raises his voice over the children or makes a joke of the disruption.' **Felicity**

# Car travel

Car travel can be easier than air travel as at least it is up to you when you stop for a break. You may want to pack a bag similar to the hand luggage you would take on an aeroplane so that you have small snacks, wet wipes, nappies and toys close to hand. Keep a change of clothes handy. CLB mum Pauline recommends travel games: 'For the under-threes try an adapted I spy … something green, something that goes "moo", etc.; who will be the next person to see a … red car, etc.; or make some big cards with pictures of things that might be seen out of the car window (e.g. sheep, lorry, church) and let your child hold them and try to spot the items one by one.'

## Mums' Top Tips

❁ 'If you take a special toy and blanket in the car, make sure they *stay in the car* when you get to your destination! You can wrap the bear or toy up in the blanket and explain that teddy is looking after the car until it's time to go home.' **Dawn**

❁ 'One of my children has always been travel-sick, but when they're under two there's nothing you can give them – just avoid too much milk. The best travel sickness remedy I have found, with the fewest side-effects, is Kwells Kids (for over-threes).' Kate

❁ 'If the children can be outside in the garden (and not in front of the television) while you pack the car, then they will be less fidgety on the journey. Take healthy snacks for the car, such as a box of raisins, and a drink. Try not to let potty-trained children drink too much or you'll be stopping every half hour!' **Dawn**

❀ 'When my babies were about eight months old we went on our first long driving trip from London to Sheffield. I was used to the children nodding off in the car, so little did I realise that most of this time they'd be awake and very dissatisfied! Having no tapes or CDs to hand – and radio stations don't exactly hit the spot until you're about eight years old and a big Kylie fan – I had to sing nursery rhymes for four hours! You might be sick of your child's Early Learning Centre CDs, but they're better than singing yourself hoarse!' **Kate**

## ▓ Mum-to-Mum: *Road trip*

### Query

*'My husband and I are driving up to see my parents at the weekend, but unfortunately they live 12 hours away. We plan on doing the trip over two days, but does anyone have any hints and tips on how to keep a 20-month-old (and her parents) from going crazy? I think my other little one, 16 weeks old, will be fine but I'm really worried that our toddler is going to go nuts in the car seat for that long.'* **Serena**

### Answers

'Last year we went on a four-hour car journey and our son was an absolute nightmare. On our next trip, we are planning to leave after lunch so that our toddler and baby can both sleep on the way (hopefully!). We don't have a front airbag, so our baby will be in the front and I'm sitting in the back with our son to help keep him amused. For the journey I'm packing books, colouring pens and pads, and little treats. Hubby is also taking earplugs, so that tantrums, which were a problem last time, won't distract him from driving!' **Gemma**

'Long car journeys are never a joy, but if you pack plenty to keep the kids amused and have goodies and make pit-stops, it should be just about bearable! Take a kiddies' music CD or an audiobook. I got the *We're Going on a Bear Hunt* CD from my local library, and it's excellent for car journeys. You can also buy purpose-made travel activity/puzzle books, which are designed to be used for long car journeys. They have little mazes and invisible-ink colouring-in and all sorts of cool stuff to keep children amused. Also, have you seen travel sticker books? These are technically for two years plus, but you could maybe get away with it?' **Fee**

'We had one long car journey that was saved by a petrol station pit-stop where we bought a cheap and tacky Barbie-doll thing. Our daughter undressed it, dressed it, and then discovered that its legs popped on and off, as well as its head, so she literally spent a good hour-and-a-half putting the head back on, legs back on and then pulling them off again. Bit grim, but it did pass the time brilliantly!' **Anna**

**Gina says:** As you can see from the advice of the CLB mums, the key to a successful road trip is to be organised, and of course make sure you give yourself plenty of time so that you can take breaks when necessary. If your car journey is more than a couple of hours long you might find it easiest to travel at 6.30/7pm. Then you can follow your usual bathtime/bedtime routine but just put him 'to bed' in the car. Most contented little babies will sleep well enough this way, and you'll arrive at your destination without having to do stops for feeds and meals. Once you reach your journey's end make sure that all the lights are kept dim and that your baby is settled quickly and with the minimum of fuss in their bed for the night. If your baby is under six months and still has a late feed, this is a great way to settle him. Be aware that your baby may be more tired than usual the next day, but if you start your day at 7am and try to keep things low-key, allowing extra rest time, he will quickly adjust.

## Planning a holiday

Sometimes the prospect of travelling with young children can feel so daunting that it is tempting not to go anywhere at all. If you find it enough of a challenge to manage things at home, you might wonder how you would ever cope elsewhere. But if you are brave and give it a go, you'll find that there is nothing more confidence-boosting than realising that your little family unit can go wherever it likes.

If going abroad is too daunting, consider a break in the UK. A few days in a UK hotel may cost as much as a week abroad, but it's more relaxing – no baggage handlers' strikes and unfamiliar food! Bedruthan Steps Hotel (see page 202) in Cornwall, a luxury hotel that caters specially for families, is recommended by one of our CLB mums, as is the website www.luxuryfamilyhotels.com.

## Mums' Top Tips

❀ 'Our first holiday with a baby was in a self-catering apart-ment; it was lovely, but quite basic, and we ended up boiling bottles as there was no microwave! The next time we went away, I researched more thoroughly and found somewhere with a washing machine, which meant I could still do a bit of washing while we were away and this cut down the amount of work for me on our return home!' **Claire**

❀ 'I have just booked our holiday for next year using a website called BabyGoes2 (see page 200). I used a stan-dard travel agent last year and had to spend ages finding a destination that catered for babies. But this site features holidays in Portugal, Greece, Corsica, Spain, the Maldives, Mauritius and Barbados, amongst others. All destinations offer kids' crèches and clubs.' **Nina**

❀ 'Book with an airline that offers you extra luggage for a baby or pre-book excess baggage – it's much cheaper than paying when you check in.' **Kelly**

❀ 'We took a cruise all around the Caribbean when our son was 22 months. It's not the sort of thing we would normally go for, but we wanted something easy and all-inclusive. The child facilities were brilliant and they had a phone intercom system so we could go to dinner and listen in to the room.' **Wendy**

❀ 'I took my baby to Spain when he was six months old. I stuck to the routine as much as I could without restricting what we did on our holiday. I always put him down for his lunchtime nap and we just sunbathed on the balcony. During the evening I would bathe and feed him as usual then head out for our meal with him in the pram at the time he was due to go to sleep. Most nights he slept in the pram, then we just popped him into his cot when we got back to the villa. Some naps went to pot and sometimes he woke up when we were out, but he was happy, so we were too. Once home, it was business as usual and we had no problems.' **Kelly**

## Preparing and packing

The best tip, I think, comes from CLB mum Emma, who says don't try to take the world with you on holiday. Do some investigation so that you know what you can buy at your destination. You don't want to take up valuable suitcase space with nappies! Hire whatever else you need (cot, highchair, etc.) online. Karen also gave us her top tips: Take lots of blackout lining; and if the hotel doesn't have a highchair, buy a travel one. She got a brilliant fabric tie-type arrangement on eBay, which slips over a chair and secures the baby.

Sallerina told us about a fabulous website called Tiny Tots Away (see page 201), which allows parents of little ones to pre-order absolutely everything they could possibly need for a holiday, either abroad or in this country. The items are delivered direct to your hotel or apartment. This company offers everything from nappies and bubble bath to formula milks and a complete range of food, together with disposable bibs and bottles. There is obviously a delivery charge, but Sallerina found it was a small price to pay for having everything organised and delivered for you so you don't have to worry about packing it.

## Mums' Top Tips

❀ 'We went on holiday when our baby was 15 weeks old. The most important thing I learnt was to start writing a list as soon as you know you are going away. Keep it by your bed: quite often I'd wake up and think, "Oh, I must put that on the list," and then by morning I had completely forgotten!' **Kelly**

❀ 'I have a packing list on the computer that I just update when needed.' **Alison**

❀ 'My tips are to get passport photos done in a shop – it's much easier than in a booth. Speak to your tour operator and see what they can arrange for you with the hotel. Our adviser managed to arrange a cot, a steam steriliser and a kettle, although none of this was in the brochure. If you have the space, start laying things out approximately a week before you go, so you can clearly see what you have got. Take medicines with you, i.e. Calpol and teething gel/powders, as well as plenty of formula. On one holiday we were told an equivalent of Cow & Gate would be available, but it was extremely expensive and gave our little one constipation.' **Kelly**

❀ 'I always take a seat for my little one as it's not always easy to get a highchair when you're out and about in cafés and restaurants.' **Sarah**

❀ 'If you're going somewhere sunny, take something to block the sun from your little one's eyes in the buggy: a parasol or a blackout cover that blocks out UV sunrays. You can get disposable steriliser bags if you need them, but you need a microwave; otherwise those cold-water steriliser tablets are fine.' **Sophie**

❀ 'Take a length of blackout fabric, so that you can black out your little one's room. Also Grobags so that they have something familiar in the travel cot.' **Liz**

❀ 'I suggest taking disposable bibs. The first time we went abroad I didn't really think about it and just threw my daughter's dirty bibs in with the washing – when we got home a week later they were all mouldy. Or you could take a plastic/wipe-clean variety.' **Holly**

❀ 'My baby was not particularly attached to any soft toys, so we just took his favourite books and a few toys to keep him amused in the car. With hindsight, though, we should have taken a soft toy to make him feel more at home at night.' **Janie**

### CLB Mums' Top 10 Best Things ... to Take on Holiday

1. Lightweight pushchair

2. Grobag

3. Monitor and room thermometer

4. Formula

5. Calpol/Nurofen

6. Cleaning brush for bottles

7. Pop-up UV tent

8. Inflatable ring for pool/sea

9. UV sunsuit and hat

10. Fitted sheet for the cot (hotels just use flat sheets, which can easily come up)

And CLB mum Pauline gave us these great tips for toddlers …

- Portable potty: take the kind that has bags with an absorbent pad inside. These are brilliant for emergency stops, avoiding dirty toilets, and are particularly good for travel sickness.

- Small plug-in nightlight (with adaptor if you are abroad): obviously you can't leave the door ajar in a hotel, and sometimes leaving the light on in the en-suite means you have to listen to the extractor fan all night.

- Emergency bath plug: you can buy large rubber circles that cover the drain, allowing you to turn a shower into a shallow bath. Some young children just don't like showers and if your room/apartment/cottage has no bath, these can rescue the night-time routine.

## Feeding on holiday

Feeding a baby on holiday is perhaps one of the greatest concerns, but our well-travelled mums have come up with some great tips, below.

### Mums' Top Tips

❁ 'Try pre-sterilised bottles, called Steribottles, which are available from supermarkets. They come in two sizes – one with a faster teat and bigger bottle. If you are planning to use them, try them out on your little one before you go away.' **Wendy**

❁ 'I took my hand-blender on holiday. I know this sounds mad, but it was a real help.' **Helen**

❁ 'On a recent trip to the States, I was concerned about how I would keep the bottles chilled throughout the journey which, door to door, took 15 hours. After looking at many bottle insulators/coolers, I found that the longest bottles could be chilled for was six hours. After many hours debating what to do, I found the perfect solution: pre-sterilised disposable bottles and small one-feed cartons of formula. This solved both the problem of keeping empty bottles fresh, as they only stay sterile for four hours, and the need for chilling. The sealed cartons need no refrigeration and can be served at room temperature. I also took enough with us to use on day trips out, which was a good job as, believe it or not, they were unavailable in the States.' **Jaz**

✿ 'When I'm travelling I prepare my bottles with the water and then add pre-measured powder as and when from one of those powder containers. If the baby doesn't get too used to having very warm milk, you'll find the milk doesn't even need to be warmed, as it's already at room temperature.' **Sharon**

✿ 'In Europe the supermarkets stock Evian water for making feeds and another brand called Fontel, which says on the side in English that it is suitable for making baby feeds.' **Kelly**

✿ 'In Spanish supermarkets there is a brand of water called Regas (Font del Regas), which has the lowest mineral content for babies' bottles.' **Joanne**

✿ 'I made a chicken casserole and a leek soup while I was away, froze them in small portions, and gave that to my son most days (take some small plastic containers and a hand-blender if you decide to do this). I found it helped to take a small number of jars and ready-made milk cartons with me, so I wasn't stressing about getting to the supermarket when I got there. But there is obviously a limit to how much you can take!' **Alison**

✿ 'When I was making each batch of frozen food in the weeks running up to our holiday, I froze one meal-sized portion into its own small bag, and then put them all into a bag marked "holiday bag" so that we had at least one of each meal to take with us. The meals survived the five-hour journey. I used ice packs and a cool bag.' **Jooles**

✿ 'I always take a very good cooler bag packed with food from home that I know my little one will eat, like cheese, sausages, fish fingers, chicken goujons, home-made shepherd's pie and bolognese, small pasta shapes, cheese sauce and tomato sauce, as well as age-appropriate ready-made milk. I check the cooler bag in as another piece of luggage. I do end up taking quite a bit, but I get stressed if I can't get things in the Spanish supermarkets.' **Sarah**

✿ 'We go to Barcelona and never pack more than an overnight bag when self-catering because we know there is a big supermarket near to where we stay.' **Riab**

✿ 'For my baby's lunches on holiday I am taking So Baby food (see page 201). They pack it frozen for you, so you just put it in the freezer when you arrive and cook from frozen each day. In the day you would probably be out and about, so should be able to heat it in the restaurants. The

Spanish are not as fussy as English restaurants about heating food.' **Sukhi**

## Holiday health

If children won't wear a hat and sunglasses, keep them in the shade as much as possible and remember that water reflects the sun, so you can get burnt in the shade if you're by water. You can treat mild sunburn by bathing with cool (not ice) water and giving Calpol or ibuprofen, but sunburn in under-ones can be more serious than it looks, so get a doctor's advice. Take the medicines you're most likely to need, including your child's regular medication, such as an asthma inhaler. Don't forget: Calpol, teething gel, nappy rash cream, digital thermometer, insect repellent and antihistamine cream. Check that all the products you're taking are suitable for your child's age. Always find out the phone number for medical emergencies for the country you're going to before you get there. Once you get to your resort/village/hotel, make sure you know how to find a doctor and pharmacy from day one.

If you're travelling to Europe, make sure you have a European Health Insurance Card (EHIC) for all family members, including your baby. This gives you state-provided healthcare at a reduced cost or sometimes free of charge. You can apply for the card, which is valid for up to five years, on the official EHIC website (www.ehic.org.uk). The card might not cover everything that would be free on the NHS, but it does entitle you to the same treatment as a resident of the country you're visiting.

## Mums' Top Tips

❀ 'Put sun cream all over your baby while they are naked in your hotel room. This makes sure there are no missed areas.' **Kelly**

❀ 'We bought a ladybird insect repellent from JoJo Maman Bébé (see page 201). You clip it on to the cot at night or the buggy when you are out and it stops the child getting bitten. Fantastic – not one bite!' **Amber**

❀ 'It's worth investing in one of those baby sun tents as it keeps them safely out of the sun when you're on the beach – but do make sure it doesn't get too hot inside.' **Sammy**

❀ 'I always take one of those little battery-operated fans when we go away as it's great for cooling down babies if it gets too hot.' **Pia**

❀ 'When our daughter started crawling, she kept putting stones and sand in her mouth. We bought an extra wind-break to make an enclosed spot for us all on the beach and covered the sand inside with towels and blankets.' **Erica**

## CLB Mums' Top 10 Best Tips ... for
## Travelling by Plane

1. A baby-sling is very useful for getting on and off the plane because it keeps your hands free.

2. We took our toddler's car seat on the plane. She was in a familiar and comfortable seat and slept most of the way there.

3. Be prepared to taste all bottles of pre-boiled water at airport security. I took a small plastic cup so that I could pour a bit from each into the cup so as not to contaminate the bottles.

4. Pack a carry-on bag with all the stuff you will need for at least 24 hours after arrival in case your bags go missing.

5. Always pack more than you need – we had a four-hour delay. Thankfully we had packed extra but I only just had enough milk, the muslins were filthy (our baby was sick) and she was looking pretty grotty in her one spare change of clothes!

6. Consider taking a change of clothes for yourself as well as your baby in your hand luggage. Spending a flight smelling of baby sick is very unpleasant!

7. Accept that you won't be able to see the movie or read a book; take some bubbles to amuse your little one.

8. I shopped for clothes for the journey in the charity shops. That meant I could bag and bin the dirty items, rather than having to carry them around for hours.

9. If you're flying long-haul and your baby is small enough to sleep in a bassinet, remember you will have very little room for yourself, and no table to eat from. It's best to be mentally prepared for the cramped conditions, and for the fact that your baby must be removed from the bassinet every time turbulence occurs.

10. Allow your toddler to walk as much as possible in the terminal. This will help tire them out before the flight.

## ■ Mum-to-Mum: *Long-haul flights and jet lag*

### Query

*'I am travelling to the US. Any tips on how can I help my 10-month-old baby to go back to her CLB routines and cope with jet lag?'* **Ghaida**

### Answers

'If you are travelling across a number of time zones, trying to stick rigidly to a routine may spoil your own holiday and that of other people. In these cases, try to relax and be flexible and remember that it will not be difficult to recover your own routines when back in familiar surroundings.' **Pauline**

'When you land, just get into the routine as it would fit in that time zone. Be aware, though, that it will take a few days for your baby's body clock to adjust, as it will yours, so allow for that and accept that there will be a few wake-ups in the night.' **Karina**

'I found we needed to go with the flow and be prepared to use different techniques to settle our baby if he woke in the night.' **Sarah**

'When you are flying with a baby, I would really advise to not worry overly about the routine – everything tends to go out of the window when you are surrounded with so many people and the baby is taking it all in and it's best not to beat yourself up about it.' **Anna**

**Gina says:** I always advise that parents try to change to the new time zone as quickly as possible. By doing this I have always found that my babies adapted in a couple of days. Accept that your baby's sleep may be a little disrupted, as this is normal when crossing time zones, but by starting each day at 7am (regardless of what's happened in the night) and sticking as closely as possible to his normal routine, this should be minimised.

## Take-off and landing

It is common for babies to cry on take-off and landing due to the change in the cabin's air pressure. Here's some advice from CLB mums to help your baby hold back the tears:

### Mums' Top Tips

❀ 'Have a dummy or a drink for the baby to suck on during take-off and landing; this helps the ears to clear.' **Yvonne**

❀ 'Try to get your baby to drink milk or water on take-off and landing.' **Anna**

❀ 'If your baby is not due a feed on take-off or landing, a drink of juice or a dummy would do the trick.' **Jaz**

## In-flight entertainment

So you've managed to get your little one on to the plane; now how do you keep him entertained for several hours? Here are some of the best CLB mum tips:

### Mums' Top Tips

❀ 'Don't take toys with little bits that easily fall on the floor and get lost. A small number of colouring pencils or crayons is great: a bumper pack will just end up under everyone else's seats.' **Kate**

❀ 'I take crayons and paper pad; glitter pens; stickers; magnetic sketcher; magnet play scene; books.' **Anna**

❀ 'I bought some Teletubbies Aqua Mats. They are about A5 size and you just fill the pen up with water and colour in the Teletubbies. This honestly kept my daughter occupied for such a long time as, obviously, the water evaporates and you can start again. My lifesaver on flights is snacks. I really think that for that one flight it just doesn't matter; anything to keep them happy – she also played with the packets afterwards.' **Lyndsay**

❀ 'It's worth wrapping all the bits you take in cheap paper because it kills another minute or so per item and provides a bit more entertainment playing with the paper! Before long-haul flights I go to a car-boot sale and spend £5–10 on bits my daughter hasn't seen before. This way you can just use them on holiday and then leave them there.' **Hannah**

❀ 'A portable DVD player was a godsend for our 19-month-old daughter, but she wouldn't keep the headphones on at all so I ended up taking them off and having the volume just loud enough for her to hear. Strangely enough she also enjoyed watching the programmes on the in-flight screen without any sound!' **Karen**

❁ 'Suction toys that can be stuck to the window or tray table often work well. Don't take noisy toys, unless you want to be the most unpopular person on the flight!' **Pauline**

❁ 'The most effective thing was discovering any other children similar in age, or even a baby, and ask their parents if your toddler can pester them for a while: they eyeball each other for ages – soooooo funny!' **Leanne**

## Getting used to a strange room

While adults are frequently energised by change and novelty, babies, of course, thrive on the familiar, so introducing an element of 'home from home' is the key to a successful holiday. Getting a reasonable night's sleep is also important – for the whole family! You're unlikely to get a lie-in on holiday, but it is preferable not to have to rise at the same time as the sun. Rather than ransacking the bathroom to cover the bedroom windows with towels, we have some great ideas for how to make the room dark enough for your little one to sleep just as he does at home.

### Mums' Top Tips

❁ 'We use bin liners and masking tape! Always works and from the outside you can't tell, as it's just black. The lengths we will go to for a good night's sleep.' **Judi**

❀ 'Faced with the challenge of covering a Velux window in a holiday cottage, my hubby disappeared to the shops to return with tinfoil and Blu-tack. Just tear off lengths of foil and stick to the window with Blu-tack and it keeps almost all the light out. It does look a bit weird when people see the window from the outside, but it has kept our daughter fast asleep until 7am as usual.' **Louise**

❀ 'I've just been away in a caravan and took some black card and stuck this to the windows with Sellotape. The card slipped into the suitcase lid, so no extra space was needed in the luggage.' **Claire**

❀ 'Take your baby's (unwashed) cot sheets and sleeping bag, if you use one, to put in a travel cot when you get there. If you have ever used Karvol plug-ins when your baby's had a cold, take these with you, as they are great at masking any strange house smells and gives them a good night's sleep – which we found to our delight on our last holiday. Our baby slept from 7pm to 7am, just like he does at home.' **Vicky**

❀ 'There's a mattress especially for babies, which is designed to keep baby's smell. It's called Mantraxx Junior by Prémaxx, a Belgian baby brand. It's flat and you can roll it up and take with you on holiday to create a familiar atmosphere, and make a strange room smell like home. It worked well with my first son, as he often visited grand-parents alone when I was pregnant.' **Gisela**

## ■ Mum-to-Mum: *Camping trip*

### Query

*'Not sure anyone is as nutty as us but we want to buy a super-cool family tent and go camping this summer with our daughter. Not sure about taking Baby Two – may have to leave her behind with Granny. Just wondered if anyone had tent or camping gear recommendations and any tips in general.'* **Fee**

### Answers

'The main thing is to make sure *you* choose the site and *you* put up the tent, as I left it to my hubby once. He and a friend chose this beautiful spot with a breathtaking view across the lake, but it was about a 10-minute walk from the car (carrying everything!) and once we got there they had put the tent up on a slight slope that didn't look that steep, until we tried to sleep and we all nearly rolled into the lake! Apart from finding a very flat plot, look for shade. And don't try to rough it – get a lovely blow-up mattress!' **Mags**

'We took our one-and-a-half-year-old to the Big Chill Festival. It was fab – hard work but hilarious. Be prepared for no sleep the first night, but lots the next – the excitement on night one is too much, but by night two everyone is shattered. Buy as big a tent as you can afford and definitely go with blow-up beds and lots of snuggly sleeping bags and duvets if you can – even in summer the ground can be very cold and the cold comes up through the mattresses very quickly. Most of all, enjoy it and be prepared to laugh!' **Jasmine**

'If you've bought a new tent, practise putting it up in your garden before you go; take a travel potty and liners for night-time, even if your children are well past potty-training age; get a "gazebo" to provide you with a shelter to eat under; and remember most campsites will allow you to re-freeze your ice packs for a small charge to keep your food cool. Don't forget your corkscrew and torch!' **Kate**

## Hiking with a baby

Our CLB mums show that it is possible to continue having adventurous and active holidays, even with a baby. Always make sure that you are fully prepared and accept that you will have to be flexible – i.e. activities you did before are likely to take longer with a baby on board so give yourself plenty of time. If you haven't tried adventurous activities before, such as mountain climbing or going on long treks, don't try them for the first time with your baby.

## Mums' Top Tips

❀ 'We bought the Macpac Possum. I really recommend the neck-roll because when you walk and they sleep, it stops their head shaking around all the time. The Macpac also stands up when on the floor, but I think it's always better to stand it against something. It has a sling at the bottom to put your foot on when taking your baby out of the carrier so that the carrier stays on the floor, and a sling at the top to lift it up more easily. Looking at some pictures of older children in them, it seems you really can use them up to two-and-a-half years – if you want to carry them!' **Kat**

❀ 'We go out quite a bit for a walk with our daughter in a back carrier; the most I've done is one-and-a-half hours with her in the back carrier. I had to stop to give her some water, but other than that she had a brilliant time. She loves it, and squeaks most of the way. My back carrier is the Bushbaby Lite, which fits anyone from around 5 to 6 ft. It's good as I'm 5 ft 2 in and hubby is 6 ft. We got the sun/rain canopy to go with it too.' **Carol**

❀ 'I took my six-month-old daughter up Snowdon. We left at 8.30am and were down again at 5pm, so it was a pretty long trip! I can really recommend the Macpac carriers. If you want your child to sit quite far down, the seat still stays pretty wide, so is comfy for them to sit on, while some others get narrower if you let them down on the strap. You should buy a Sleepyhead or neck-roll, too, and the rain or sun cover works a treat. Our baby "enjoyed" climbing up Snowdon and slept a lot during that, but downhill she didn't like it. Because it was quite steep and my husband had to lean forward to climb down some bits, she was often pressed against the front of the carrier, like in a roller-coaster just going over the first edge! So I can recommend long hikes, but maybe not too steep! We took a travel bottle-warmer and thermos with us, and a UV sunhat with a flap to cover her neck.' **Kat**

✿ 'We just got back from a trip to Nova Scotia, Canada, where we did lots of hiking. Our daughter loved it! The carrier we used is called Kelty Kids and I'd definitely recommend it. It is light, easy to pack up, has lots of pockets and stands when you put it down. The longest hike we went on was about three hours. I can't wait to do it again!' **Jane**

✿ 'We were still using Macpac carriers when our daughters were three years old! The only problem – apart from their weight – is that they do that small-child thing of wanting to get in and out of the carrier along the way, which can make progress quite slow!' **Kate**

## Summary – points to remember

● Make the effort to go out during the day – it can be all too easy to find excuses not to. A short trip to the park or the local shops, especially if you're walking, will lift your mood, and meeting other parents locally can be a lifeline.

● Keep that baby bag stocked in the hallway or car to make getting out quicker and easier.

● If you cannot organise an outing around your routine, remember that a few disruptions will make very little difference for one day: you'll be back on track tomorrow.

● Holidays with very young children are very different from the holidays you took when you were childless. Despite this, a week's freedom from your job, and the responsibilities of the home and relationships outside your partner and children, does give you a new perspective, leaving you refreshed.

● Good planning is essential, but try not to over-plan every aspect of your break, as you will be exhausted before you go.

● Keep your packing list on the computer so that you can just update it for each trip.

● It's good to be mentally (and practically) prepared for such things as flight delays or illness – or even just an episode of teething – but try not to become too anxious about things going wrong. A holiday is not just a series of problems to be encountered!

- When packing hand luggage, anticipate delayed flights and temporarily lost luggage. Take extra muslins, formula and spare clothes, but be sure to check anything you're uncertain of (such as dimensions and weight of hand luggage) with the airline before you pack.

- What you take in terms of formula/food for your little one depends partly on your character and how adaptable your child is. If you feel more comfortable taking the contents of your local supermarket to Spain, do it. It's more important that you feel as relaxed as possible than what other people think of you.

- If you have the means, try a company like So Baby or Tiny Tots Away, which will organise baby necessities – particularly food – for your holiday.

- Pre-sterilised bottles, ready-made formula and disposable bibs are handy for holidays.

- If you're self-catering and need to make purées, take your hand-blender (and adaptor if you're going abroad) – you won't regret it!

- Take something to black out bedroom windows.

- Favourite snacks and a few inexpensive, well-chosen new toys are the secret to a happy flight with a toddler.

- Don't forget the Calpol and antihistamine cream.

# 5

# Going Back to Work or Being a Full-Time Mum

Becoming a mum is the beginning of a new life. Where once your days were probably filled with thoughts of work, for the first few months of your baby's life you are more likely to be preoccupied with feeds and nap times than with filing or schedules. However, once your baby is in a good routine, you may well begin to consider whether and when to go back to work.

For many mothers this can be a confusing time, and all the ideas and plans you had before the baby's birth can change dramatically. As one career mum, Ahutukel, says: 'Even before I got pregnant I always thought that when I had a baby I would go back immediately and focus on my career again as soon as I could, but now I just feel the opposite way.' For many mums, whether or not to return to work is one of the hardest and most heart-wrenching decisions of their child's early life. It's that 'head and heart' thing. As Ahutukel says: 'My mind says if I don't start now, I will miss the opportunities and even if I do want to go back after a couple of years, I won't be able to find a good job, and they will prefer someone who hasn't taken a career break. But my heart tells me something different. Even when I think about not being able to see my children properly for five whole days, I just feel heartbroken. I never thought I would be like that, but I really enjoy taking care of our children, house and social life, and I know that I definitely improved my family's quality of life after I stopped working, and that gives me satisfaction.'

Mother of twins, Louise, sums up the feelings of mothers everywhere: 'I'm struggling to accept that when you have kids your life changes! I don't quite know what I thought was going to happen, but I guess until the reality of babies arrives you think you can carry on in your own merry little way.'

One thing is certain: your working life will never be the same again once you have children. Whether you choose to return to work full-time or part-time, if you work from home or are taking time to study, you no longer have only yourself to consider. Many mothers find that this makes them more productive at work. Knowing that they must collect their baby from childcare at a set time, and keen as they are to see their little ones again, mothers tend to work with the same efficiency and level of organisation with which they run their home lives. This is just one of the many benefits of work, extolled by mums everywhere.

While being a working mum brings many new challenges, there are ways that these can be tackled. Our CLB mums have heaps of suggestions on how to cope with the practicalities as well as the more emotional aspects of going back to work. Although it's an agonising decision to take, in fact the modern mum is able to juggle career and motherhood in a way that would have been unthinkable for previous generations. This is due to so many things, including technology (think of all those mothers working at home while their baby naps, linked to the world by their laptop), easy-care fabrics (much less ironing!), the wide availability of easy-to-cook food (gone are the days of having to grow your own vegetables and knead your own bread – although I would strongly recommend that you do both of these if you have the chance), and, importantly, the widespread provision of excellent childcare. So, armed with a list of nurseries and questions to ask potential childminders, mothers set off to find the ideal place for their little one. To make things a little easier, in this section I have gathered some very useful suggestions on what to look for in a nursery or childminder.

The thought of leaving their precious newborn with strangers, be it with a childminder or at a nursery, can cause even the most ambitious career-driven mother to have doubts, and a baby's first day in childcare leaves most mothers in tears. However, the fact that at the end of the day there is a happy, smiling baby, who is delighted to see you, can dissolve many of the anxieties. As mum Clare points out, 'It is hard work but I know Jack is in safe hands, and when I pick him up from nursery he is *so* excited to see me. Then when we get home we have a nice time, a little play and fun in the bath and getting ready for bed.'

Initial worries about whether a nursery is capable of looking after your little one and maintaining his routines are natural and understandable, but the advice I have collected on this topic shows that many CLB mums have felt exactly the same, and have some extremely positive things to say on the matter.

But of course not all women go back to work once their baby is six months old. There is a growing band of mothers who choose to stay at home, often taking a break from enjoyable and fulfilling careers, in order to spend time with their little ones in the pre-school years. This is never an easy option. Fee, mother of two children under the age of three, speaks for many: 'I feel incredibly housebound at the moment and restricted and I am always here staring at the same walls. I find being a stay-at-home mum doesn't make me totally happy. I find it incredibly difficult at times. It is very repetitive and tiring and I often feel lonely and isolated. I miss contact with people from work and the stimulation work provided.' In fact, being a stay-at-home mother and caring for children is often described by mums as the hardest job they have ever done. However, whatever their reasons for choosing this path, most mums find a way to enjoy this lifestyle, and I have gathered together a host of their life-enhancing suggestions.

Whatever the outcome of your deliberations regarding

work and childcare, I strongly urge you to feel positive about your decision and enjoy your time – be it at home with the children or in the workplace. Mum of two, Laura, hits the nail on the head, saying, 'Whatever you decide, the challenge is to do it and not feel (too) guilty. You will be doing what's best for you and, ultimately, your family. A happy mummy means a happy home.'

# Going back to work

Once the decision is made to return to work, do your best to prepare yourself for both the emotional wrench of being apart from your baby – who will have become the centre of your world – and coming to terms with the fact of someone else looking after her. This can be one of the most difficult challenges as a new mum, but you will get through it. Give yourself time to get used to the new work/life balance and don't be too hard on yourself if it's taking you some time to adjust.

Maria says, 'I've met many mums who appear effortlessly to juggle career, family, friends, the lot, and are adamant that they are coping; I have been told all it needs is a bit of confidence, creative management and a lot of "chutzpah". So what if they haven't cleaned under the cooker in years? As long as their children have memories of outings, dancing and stories with their mum, for them that's their job well done.'

It can help if you make the transition gradually and make sure you have someone with you for support on that all-important first day. CLB mum Rachel says, 'Regular visits to my son's nursery were key to settling him. We had around five visits, gradually extending the time and leaving him there alone for periods without me. I began this six months before the nursery start. This allowed more time for me to get used to the idea and my son to get used to the nursery environment. The first day I was dropping him off for real, and going back to work, was very upsetting. We allowed time for this and I was able to go for a coffee afterwards to calm myself down before going to work. I'd definitely recommend taking along your husband or a close friend or relative for support; even if it is just for a few minutes after-wards, you will be grateful for it.'

## Mums' Top Tips

❀ 'If you have the flexibility, do what makes you happiest overall. Working mums tend to feel guilty, but so do stay-at-home mums!' **Laura**

❀ 'I think if you really enjoy your job you have to go back. It would be awful if you left your job and then found later on that you couldn't get something as good. Just about the most sensible thing my health visitor has said to me is that you have to think about the long term too!' **Susie**

❀ 'I think if you are a working mum, guilt is to be expected as part of everyday life!' **Kate**

❀ 'When deciding whether to go back to work, I recommend writing a list of pros and cons … it's what I always do when I have big decisions to make and it helps me, even if I then choose to ignore my own advice and go entirely the opposite way.' **Laura**

❀ 'When I went back to work after my first baby, I felt anxious about how he would cope and how I would cope! My son went to a workplace nursery close to my husband's work and this really helped with the transition and meant my husband could sometimes visit him in his lunch hour. Keeping the connection with our baby through the working day helped me feel more relaxed about him and therefore more able to concentrate on my work. I also found it really helpful that I kept breastfeeding. I loved coming home at the end of the day and lying on the bed to feed him. It felt like a great way to re-connect with my baby after a day apart.' **Dani**

❀ 'I'm gearing up to go back to work full-time in a few months. One thing that I keep weighing up against my sad feelings is the anticipation of a full salary again. I don't mean that to sound cold … it just helps a little!' **Rebecca**

## ■ Mum-to-Mum: *Dreading a return to work*

### Query

*'I keep having panicky moments thinking about going back to work and my baby not being a baby anymore. My partner doesn't seem to understand. I'm so scared of leaving her or missing something. She has started going to nursery for an hour twice a week to get her used to it but I still worry, and don't know how I'm going to get through the day without her. I was a nursery nurse so I know how important the environment is to a child, but that doesn't help me stop feeling this way. My little girl is growing so fast and I feel like I'm going to hardly see her.'* **Gem**

### Answers

'I feel exactly the same. I'm dreading Macey going to nursery – I wish I could stay at home all the time with her, but I know it isn't the best thing for us both long term. I need to get back to the adult world and she needs to learn to interact with other kids. Allow yourself some time to wallow and feel sorry for yourself – it will be hard but you will get through it and you will be so excited to see your baby each day after nursery that you'll spend some amazing quality time with her before bed each evening. The weekends will also be so special and you will look forward to them and the time you get to spend with her. I'm sure she will love nursery and will excitedly tell you all about it as she gets older.' **Michelle**

'It is hard but it's amazing how quickly you revert back to your former self. I found it very odd – like living in two parallel worlds, and couldn't believe how easily I could slide from one to the other. I found it a mistake to put photos up on my desk, as this upset me. I'm not denying it's hard but the thought of it is worse than the reality. Organisation-wise it's hard and I have to say I've never had such a terrible social life. I want to catch up with my little one during the weekend and not see anyone else, though luckily my partner doesn't let me become a complete hermit! I'm sure your baby will come on leaps and bounds in nursery – and think of all the pressies you can buy yourself with your salary!' **Sophie**

'Sophie is totally right – it is weird how quickly you go back to how you were. Sometimes if I am really into something at work, I forget I left at all! I have a picture of my baby on my desktop to remind me and I run into nursery to grab him!' **Rachael**

**Gina says:** I think Sally sums it up perfectly. She says, 'It's perfectly normal to feel like that. Your baby has been your world for months and now you have to go back to reality. I won't deny that I had to be carried sobbing out of the nursery by my partner on the first day, but it quickly got easier and the nursery was fabulous. They kept in contact and phoned me when my baby wouldn't settle – just knowing what was going on was great. It *will* get easier after the first week, I promise. My last bit of advice is to take plenty of vitamins as germs are so easily spread at nursery – we had seven colds in the first few months!'

## CLB Mums' Top 10 Best Tips ... for Returning to Work

1. Don't forget that all parents with children under six years old are entitled to request flexible working arrangements. This doesn't mean you are entitled to work part-time, but it does mean that your employer has to consider your proposal. If they can't accommodate your requests, they also have to confirm why, in writing.

2. Get support from others to help manage your household tasks. Buying in help may not be an option, but are there friends or family that you can barter with? Maybe you can offer them a service in return for helping you out. I know a mum in full-time work who does internet searches for a relative (something she finds easy and is done when her son is asleep) in return for babysitting. During the babysitting she catches up with all of her housework so that when she is with her son he gets all her attention.

3. Getting ready for work needs a lot more time and planning. I run through the day in my head the night before. This involves getting the bottles washed by 8pm so they can be prepared for the next day by 10pm. I did

the bottles in the morning initially and that definitely didn't work!

4. If I have to start work before 9am, I always pack my baby's bag the night before. Have a separate bag for nursery, if possible, then you don't lose your changing bag should you need it on the way back home.

5. Anyone who looks after my children (parents and in-laws included) gets a typed copy of their routine. This may seem like overkill, but it does mean that everyone knows what to expect!

6. Factor in the travelling to childcare. It is a one-hour car journey to work and the nursery is one minute from work. My baby naps in the car on the way to nursery. In the evening, I put the back interior light on and have bought car toys for my son to play with as he has cut out his afternoon nap. I also change the baby seat from a reclining position for sleep (morning) to an upright sitting position (evening). My son tends to stay awake on the way home.

7. Find ways to take the pressure off if you can. I am getting a cleaner once a week and she also does iron-ing. I will continue to shop online as it is so easy.

8. It's much easier to get used to being back at work if you can gradually build your hours up when you first go back. I did it by using some annual leave at the start and it made it less of a shock for me and my baby.

9. If you are going to be leaving your child with a nanny or childminder, I think it's really worth having an alternative emergency backup just in case there's a last-minute problem. You may have a relative who would consider this, or you could arrange mutual emergency childcare with a friend or colleague.

10. Making some time for yourself is very important as it can be so easy to rush from working all day to caring for your baby at home without any space for yourself at all. Leave a bit of time every so often to go to the gym or to have a massage or a haircut – it will make all the difference.

## Benefits of working

When you are struggling with the thought of returning to work, it can help to focus on the benefits. CLB mum, Maria, has a wonderfully positive attitude to this: 'Embrace what working is bringing. Consider what you contribute to the family, for example, when you have a family day out; enjoy the thought that it would not have been financially possible if you weren't working. Also think about the wealth of skills and experiences you are able to share with your child. You are one of, if not her main role model, so tell her about your job, why you enjoy it and why it is important to you. You will be setting her a great example.'

## Mums' Top Tips

❀ 'You have got to be true to yourself. If you are the sort of person who wouldn't be happy as a full-time mother, you will be a better mother to your children if you work, because you will be a happier person overall.' **Kelli**

❀ 'I spent my first few shifts in a daze but now I actually quite enjoy going to work part-time. I feel like I have the best of both worlds – still "my life" and a family life.' **Amy**

❀ 'Some mornings when I get my baby up and she's being super-grumpy, I'm actually glad to drop her off at nursery and I really enjoy my time apart from her (and the fact she seems to love nursery helps, too!).' **Laura**

❀ 'When I go out in the mornings I know it is an easier job waiting for me!' **Debs**

❀ 'Remember the benefits of your baby being in childcare. I think it's very good for children's social development to spend time with other children.' **Susie**

❀ 'Remember what you're contributing and imagine the impact on the economy if all mums decided to stop work.' **Kirsten**

❀ 'I think it's quite important that my children see that their mummy has a job and that my job is not cleaning the house. I know this is a controversial view but I feel it's one worth mentioning.' **Louise**

❀ 'I almost think it will do me good to hand my baby over and let someone else do the job for a couple of days and for me to get stuck into my other day job.' **Kay**

❀ 'Stop worrying about what's happening when you're not with your baby and savour the moment when you can have that uninterrupted coffee!' **Christina**

## Making work work

I was inspired to read Dani's experience. She said that throughout the years of having children and working, it had always helped her to remember why it is that she works, what her purpose is and to remember that through working she has helped to provide a better quality of life for her children, as well as contributing to the world in other ways. It helped her to talk through any guilt she had about leaving the children and remember the ways in which she was a good mother, and that working and earning money made her a responsible mother.

CLB mum Maria's approach is to accept your decision and get on with it: 'If you need to work for the money, don't dwell on this any longer as it is a definite, and unless you find a job that has more money for fewer hours, your situation isn't going to change. On those inevitable days when work is not enjoyable, it is worth considering that sometimes just getting on with things can be the best way of getting through. Spending time on "what ifs" instead of moving forward is wasted time that you don't have.'

## Mums' Top Tips

✿ 'I find it helpful to have nice things planned to do with my baby on the days I'm not working. This helps to make me feel like I am making the most of the time' **Dani**

✿ 'Give it time for you both to settle into the new routine, and I guarantee within three months you'll be saying how fantastic it is to be back at work.' **Imogen**

✿ 'Although it is hard emotionally and very tiring, I honestly think that putting my baby into nursery and going back was the right decision and allowed me to devote time at work to work and time at home to being mummy.' **Rachael**

✿ 'What helped me was having "staying-in-touch days". We can have up to 10 days paid work during our maternity leave. This meant that I could keep up to date with the team and our work and that I didn't feel like a complete alien coming back to work. I only did five staying-in-touch days but it did help.' **Emma**

✿ 'The weekends are very precious to us and we often go for nice walks and picnics. I like to keep Jack in the routine as much as possible at the weekend else he tends to catch up on sleep.' **Clare**

## Work options

When you return to work after having a baby, you may need to find more flexible ways of working. The CLB mums share their experiences:

### Mums' Top Tips

✿ 'I tried to find ways to earn money from home, so that I would still have a disposable income of my own. I sat down one day and made a list of all the skills I had, and how I could possibly make money from them. I even included things such as being efficient at ironing! I finally decided to look for work as an audio-typist and to try to build a business as a portrait artist. Although I have never been formally trained in either, I have always been very quick at typing and very good at art. I contacted the local TV station and was soon working from home, transcribing their programme scripts. I also began practising drawing portraits and was soon flooded with commissions. In fact, I've been so successful at working as an artist that I gave up the audio-typing to concentrate on it solely.' **Kim**

✿ 'I started working four days a week but after five months I went down to three days a week. Even though I went back to work for financial reasons, it was important for me to get the balance between work/earning money and being with my baby. So my husband and I made some choices about having less money (and making some significant sacrifices) so that I could be with Gabriel as much as possible. Overall for me, this kept me sane and happy that I was being the mother I wanted to be as well as not missing out on my baby.' **Dani**

✿ 'I work from home, which means I have a job I enjoy, time with my lovely little boy every day before he goes to nursery and when he comes home, and the flexibility to be there for him if he is ill. People talk about "juggling" work and childcare but I don't feel that that's what I'm doing at all. I work four days a week with Wednesdays off and I really value the time before 10am, Wednesdays and weekends. I think it does make me appreciate my son more, as when he is being lovely (fortunately most of the time), I really enjoy it, and if he is being grotty then I know that someone else will be dealing with it the next day.' **Susie**

❀ 'I work my set hours and the stresses and strains that
I craved no longer appeal to me at all. Though I will look
forward to sinking my teeth back into it at a later point,
right now my priority is my baby. I know if I had any more
responsibility I would do an extra hour's work here and
there. Now I just enjoy it. I know when the time is right
I will want more children, and if my current employers
won't have me, someone else will.' **Joanne**

## ▦ Mum-to-Mum: *Working from Home*

### Query

*Just wondered if there are any of you out there who work from
home? How do you do it? How do you find the time?'* **Kasia**

### Answers

'When my daughter was seven months old, she went to nursery for two days and I worked at home for two-and-a-half
days, intending to juggle the other half day when she was
napping, and in the evenings. It didn't really work out, if I'm
honest. I often had to make and take calls while feeding or
changing a nappy. There were urgent letters that needed
writing regardless of whether it was a work day for me. I
ended up feeling as if I was short-changing my clients and
also not giving the time to my baby that she needed. It was
very difficult for me as I've always given 100 per cent to my
work and loved it. I started to resent the demand that work

was having on my time, and the intrusion it made on my time with my baby. And, when she was sleeping, I wanted to catch up on the ironing/housework, or just put my feet up! I haven't gone back since having my second baby and it's been great (most of the time!). I'm still doing some volunteer work for the charity I worked for and, next year, I'm doing some more training in counselling so I'm hoping that working in the future will be more flexible.' **Laura**

'I work from home twice a week. I work only during the lunchtime nap, but I am lucky as my baby normally sleeps for two hours. The only way I can do it is by setting a basic rule: when I need to work, I just sit and do that – no cleaning, cooking, etc. In order to do so, though, I need to have the house clean enough to be able to concentrate only on my work. As soon as my baby is in bed (11.45am), I turn on the computer and normally manage to work from 12.30 to 2pm. Longer than that is really hard. Then of course there is the 7 to 10pm slot, but you need to have a full sleep to be still "alive" by then! My advice would be only start working when you have the energy to do it.' **Luisa**

'I tried to work from home, but it wasn't successful. I ended up doing one hour a day during the lunchtime nap and if it went wrong then I did it in the evening, and if my baby didn't settle then that was it. Even with a fantastic routine like ours, I always think there are no guarantees with babies and the many days or evenings I have planned but failed to work have proved this. Although it is hard emotionally and very tiring, I honestly think that putting my son into nursery and going back was the right decision. I would say if you can get some-one to have the baby for the day then do that.' **Rachael**

'I was self-employed and started work again when my baby was six months old. I'm a translator and I have to concen-trate fully; it's definitely not a job you can do with a baby or toddler around, or just fit into nap-times, especially as nap-times get shorter. My baby goes to nursery four days a week. I absolutely do not do any work when he is at home. I really think that childcare is the way to go, as then you have a clear distinction between work and non-work time. I also think it's very good for children's social development to spend time with other children.' **Susie**

'I have worked from home since my baby was just short of three months old. The biggest problem I found was that I was never just an office worker (as I had my baby with me) and never just a mum (as at home I was working part of the day). By the time she was eight months I decided she was old enough to start daycare and she loves it. I love my work and now Sarah has settled into care I am really enjoying it. I am expressing milk to give Sarah breast milk at daycare and when I give that up at 12 months I will feel totally normal again!' **Skye**

**Gina says:** If you're looking after a baby and trying to work at home, you have to be super-organised and disciplined with your routine, and a little bit of help doesn't go amiss. Here's a breakdown of busy CLB mum Kim's day: 'I work my day by being up, showered and dressed by 8.30am and have the kids dressed and breakfasted by 9am at the latest. Kai goes for a nap at 9/9.15am until 9.45/9.50am. During this time Corey munches toast on the sofa while watching CBeebies and I sit at the table and work. We then go to mums and tots or whatever in the morning, Kai goes to bed at 12.15pm, Corey sleeps on the sofa usually and I work until about 2pm. We then play until 3pm, at which time I have a nanny who comes in until 5pm. I usually get to work for a total of four hours per day, which means I do get quite a lot done. If you can find someone who could come in to help out with the kids, it makes life a lot easier.'

## Your partner's role

You and your partner may decide that it is better for him to stay at home full-time or work part-time, especially if you are the main breadwinner. If you are in a situation where you are both working, it is essential to share the care: counsellors suggest that having firm roles within a relationship can help to create harmony. It's when these roles are undefined that blame and a shortfall in expectations can emerge. It's something that

Rebecca became aware of in her relationship: 'Things wouldn't get done or would get done twice over because we had never agreed whose responsibility they were. I manage a team of people in the office and they all have job descriptions so I applied the same principle at home. We sat down and drew up a list of all the tasks and areas there were and divvied them up. Now, my husband knows that everything to do with the kids' education is his domain and I know everything to do with clothes (which sadly includes washing them!) is mine.'

## Mums' Top Tips

❀ 'Accept that you can't be superwoman and get your partner to share the load. We try to share the childcare handover in the mornings and evenings. I think it makes you both feel a bit more involved as you get that feedback in person from the carer. If your little one is old enough to chatter to you, you also get the benefit of being the one they can tell about their day.' **Riab**

❀ 'My partner and baby had some good "quality" time together. It was a bit difficult for him at first as I had breastfed and you do tend to hog the baby when you breastfeed. But it did them the world of good to spend so much time together. Not all fathers get this opportunity to spend so much time with their children when they are so small; I don't think he will regret it.' **Joanne**

❀ 'Understand your husband's need for some time to himself. My husband was a brilliant help to me, but always needed some time to himself at weekends.' **Marge**

# Studying

If you want to keep your brain ticking over while on maternity leave or while you're a stay-at-home mum, you could consider studying. Here are the experiences of the CLB mums:

### Mums' Top Tips

❀ 'If your evening tutorial starts at 7pm, leave the house as soon as your partner gets home – go to the library, the pub, anywhere you feel like, with your books, prior to the tutorial. That way you don't risk getting caught up in baby stuff until 10 minutes after you were supposed to leave. You have time to get your head in the right space for studying and give study time the respect it deserves.' **Abbie**

❀ 'Try to get out of the house and take your books to a café or somewhere so that you can focus and not end up doing housework instead of studying. When writing assignments, I take the laptop to my office and don't allow myself to surf the internet.' **Riab**

❀ 'Try not to let your study dominate family life. Have one day in the week that you do things as a family, and it's good to have a day off from studying.' **Marge**

# Effect on children of working

When you return to work, it's all too easy to feel guilty and then spoil your child when you do see him. As CLB mum Alison advises, try to be firm, fair and consistent because the less structure and more time her son had, the worse he behaved. She said, 'I've actually found that when we have had long spells together at home, he misses the stimulation and interaction with children his own age.'

## Mums' Top Tips

❀ 'I really believe that you should never feel guilty for working and never feel you have to make it up to your children by letting them get away with things that you otherwise wouldn't allow.' **Lucy**

❀ 'My three-year-old has learnt to share and play with other children in a way that is noticeably different from his friends who are at home all week. I think the social aspect of nursery is hugely valuable.' **Toria**

❀ 'I have two girls and, although at first I worried about the effect on them of being looked after by someone else, I think it's really important that they see that Mummy has a job that is just as important and valuable as Daddy's job.' **Sheila**

❀ 'I think it's important that you are proud of yourself for being a working mum as that way your children will be proud of you too.' **Fay**

❀ 'My son has really benefited from being at nursery. He does so much more than we ever did when I was looking after him at home as then I had to think about other things like shopping and cleaning and cooking. At nursery, he spends the whole day having fun. The staff are so creative and inventive and seem to have different things out for the children every morning – sometimes I feel I'd quite like to stay and join in myself!' **Esther**

# Finding childcare

Nursery, childminder, nanny? What's the best type of childcare and where do you begin when it comes to finding the right carer for your precious baby? The truth is that there are pros and cons to every type of childcare. You and your partner need to work out the best option for you, given your budget, your working hours and what you think would suit your child.

## CLB Mums' Top 10 Best Tips ... for
## Finding a Nursery

1.  The best nurseries tend to be fully booked and have long waiting lists of up to a year, so it's worth getting your name down as early as possible.

2.  Ask people you trust. A personal referral is worth a lot more than dozens of scheduled visits.

3.  Try to think of the things you are not going to compromise on, such as a dedicated area for sleeping. Is it the same as the conditions your baby will sleep in at home? I found this to be a big decider in my son's nursery choice as the final choice had a separate blacked-out room for babies. Some things you will have to be more flexible about, as no single nursery will meet all your needs.

4.  Remember, it's about finding the form of childcare that works best for the whole family – not just for your little one.

5.  Remember that your decision isn't final for the rest of your baby's life. You might find the ideal baby room at one nursery, but might want to switch to a different nursery with better play facilities as your child gets older.

6.  Be really clear about your baby's routine. Write everything down, with exact times and 'no-later-than's (i.e. bottle at 2.30pm, must be finished by 3.15pm, etc.). Who cares if the nursery thinks you're mad; they will love

spending time with your baby because she will carry on being contented!

7.  When selecting a nursery, look at Ofsted data online and do a thorough internet search into the nursery. Does it have a website and what does it show? This is a good point of comparison when you actually visit the premises.

8.  Take a note of everything from the start of choosing your nursery – how do the staff sound when they answer the phone, and how do the children sound in the background? How willing are they for you to make an appointment to inspect the nursery?

9.  Look carefully at the other children in the nursery: how do they seem? In the nursery I chose, the staff were smiling and sitting down on the floor playing with the babies and cuddling them. The environment was clean and so were the toys, and the babies were happy and relaxed. There was plenty of space. When you think you have decided on a nursery, visit and revisit until you are totally happy. Going at different times in the day allowed me to get a picture of the nursery and how it works at different times of the day.

10. Keep talking to the nursery and keep them on side. I have written them thank-you cards for things they have done and always thank them for looking after my son at the end of each day. As such, we have built up a good relationship and I trust them.

## Choosing a childminder

CLB mum Janie supplied this great list of questions to ask a potential childminder. She suggests making a list of these before you meet the childminder so that you don't forget anything important. She also says, 'If the childminder sounds ideal, pay them a visit – don't specify a time, just morning or afternoon. One childminder I visited just ignored my baby. Needless to say I didn't use her.' Also see the National Childminding Association website (see page 202) for its guide to choosing childcare, which includes further questions to ask.

1. Ask questions about the things you do and don't want. For example, a non-smoking environment might be essential; you might prefer there to be no pets; you might definitely want there to be a garden or other safe outdoor space for your child to play.

2. Where will the baby nap?

3. Does the childminder provide meals and, if so, what kind?

4. How many children does the childminder look after (including their own) and at what times?

5. Do they do school pick-up and drop-offs and, if so, at what times and how long are the journeys?

6. What sort of car and car seats does the childminder have?

7. Are they a member of the National Childminding Association of England and Wales?

8. What backup arrangements does the childminder have for when they are sick?

9. What activities do they plan for the children and what sorts of toys are available?

10. What is the attitude to TV/DVDs – do the children in their care only watch them occasionally or does the childminder rely on them to keep the children entertained?

11. What are their thoughts on your routine and can they roughly adhere to it?

12. Would the childminder be taking your child to other people's houses?

13. Can you speak to the people supplied as references?

## Mums' Top Tips

❀ 'Follow your instincts. If you feel something is not quite right but cannot explain why, trust yourself and go to see a different childminder.' **Janie**

❀ 'I wrote down the pros and cons (with my needs also included) and decided that individual care (as much as that is possible) with a childminder was the way forward. You need to feel confident giving instructions to the childminder and that she shares your philosophy.' **Michelle**

## ■ Mum-to-Mum: *Nursery or childminder?*

### Query

*'I would like some advice about the pros and cons of nursery versus childminder. Which would be better? I know that a childminder can't have more than one child under a year old, so my baby will not be able to spend time with other babies his own age. Can anyone offer some words of wisdom? Also, how do you get over that nervousness about leaving your baby with a stranger?'* **Kasia**

### Answers

'I like nursery because I know where my son is for the entire day and who's with him, that there's a cot for him to sleep in whenever he needs it (rather than him being out asleep in the pushchair/car, etc.) and that he's fed healthy meals. What puts me off a childminder is that she could be out and about anywhere during the day and, even if I trust the childminder, I don't know who else may visit her house or who else she may visit. The childminders at toddler groups sometimes seem more interested in having a gossip while their charges play on the floor – I'm sure this isn't the case for all but it does deter me. I hope I haven't offended any childminders, I'm sure there are some fantastic ones, but it's not for me and mine.' **Kelly**

'The reason why I settled on a nursery was that the child-minders all seemed to have a few kids of all different ages (some school/pre-school age) and I was concerned about the disruption to my baby's routine with things like school runs and playgroups. Also, I know that everyone is entitled to an "off" day (where they just can't be bothered!) or time off sick. If that person is one of a few nursery nurses in a team then there will be others to pick up her slack. If it's someone working on her own, it means the level of babycare will be adversely affected. On the upside, childminders do tend to be a bit more flexible with pick-up times and might even do babysitting. Also, your baby is likely to have a better one-to-one relationship with a childminder.' **Laura**

'I am sure a childminder will be reliable but she can ring and say she can't care for your baby, whereas a nursery will always have your baby no matter what. If staff phone in sick, they arrange for a replacement. Also, in nursery your child has others to play with, but having said that, childminders can always take them to playgroups where they can meet children the same age.' **Sam**

'My childminder is brilliant! She is Ofsted-registered and because she only has three children on the day my son is there, she spends a lot of one-on-one time with him. It's probably her I have to blame for him walking so early! She always asks me what I want her to work with him on and gives a detailed daily diary with nappy changes, activities, sleep, food. All her food is home-cooked. I can't sing her praises highly enough and she follows the routine to the letter. If she is sick or on holiday, there are two part-time childminders that she uses to step in. Also, I think it is nice that my son has a range of children of different ages to interact with.' **Debbie**

'I have a nanny. She is fantastic, but definitely more expensive than a nursery. We are both very flexible with working times, holidays, etc. when needed. She has never had a sick day and stays back for babysitting, etc. when asked. She takes my daughter to swimming and a gym class through the week and then organises other activities. I personally prefer having her look after my daughter here at home. We have a camera in our house too so we can monitor what she is doing – highly recommended if you choose to go down the nanny path. We wanted one-on-one care for our daughter, but I do think children learn faster at nursery as my friends' little ones have.' **Mel**

'The benefit of a nursery is that it is a structured environment and there is more than one person there (i.e. if someone isn't up to scratch it is noticeable and checked and that person has to report to a boss). They are regulated as well. Try to visit as many as you can – I looked at about five or six. The most expensive, plush one was in fact not good at all – no sleep room and everyone on the floor! You will get a feeling when you walk around them and after seeing a few you will know which one is right. Go with your gut instinct.' **Rachael**

**Gina says:** There is no right or wrong choice. Maybe interview some childminders and visit some nurseries and then go with what feels right. Try not to be too indecisive: don't keep changing your choice of carer as this might be disruptive for your baby. CLB mum Sophie says: 'I have used all three options! That is the worst thing possible – for goodness' sake stick with your first choice is my only advice!'

## Concerns about childcare

It's perfectly normal to worry about your choice of childcare, but in time your trust and confidence will grow. Handing over control of your baby to someone else is extremely difficult, but as time goes on, and you see that your little one is happy and contented, you will relax and get used to the new situation. CLB mum Sophie said that her little one was nearly always happy when she picked him up and he had built up a really lovely relationship with the other children and his childminder. She said, 'He often did things better for the childminder than he did for me, such as eating all his food and sitting happily on his own, and he loved the other children the childminder looked after.'

## Mums' Top Tips

❀ 'I have to say that however much you try to tell the carers about the routine, they have to be able to use their own initiative and, in reality, a full two-hour sleep after lunch is probably not always going to happen. My baby doesn't seem any the worse for it, apart from being much noisier on the nursery days when she gets home. One of the beauties of the CLB routine is that the babies seem to effortlessly slip back into it on the other days and they will associate the routine with home.' **Morgan**

❀ 'The first thing to remember is that no matter where your child goes, it will not be as good as at home with you. Nobody is going to match that environment so don't even try to look for it in another place.' **Fee**

❀ 'Things really improved once I'd sent in all the things my son had at home for sleep – his sleeping bag, his wave machine, his bedtime story, etc. and the staff try to stick to the same nap-time routine I do at home.' **Kelly**

❀ 'I made sure that the staff knew I was serious about the routine and I went through everything in detail.' **Leanne**

❀ 'At the beginning I quizzed the childminder a bit. Once I stopped doing this she started telling me more information freely, rather than looking panicked that I was going to start quoting times and routines to her. You definitely want to build up a trusting relationship with the carer and this is a two-way thing. Now I just ask whether my baby has been grizzly or happy rather than asking for exact sleep times/feed times. Instead of calculating my evening strategy based on how much sleep my baby's had, I simply judge how tired he seems.' **Kitty**

## Being prepared for illness

Many parents are shocked by how frequently their children are ill once they start nursery or pre-school, but this is nothing to worry about and is a normal part of a child's development. However, unless you are able to keep taking time off work, it makes sense to have some backup arrangements in place. Give your nursery all your contact numbers, and also those of a neighbour, or a nearby relative or friend, who could be contacted in an emergency.

CLB mum Emma has some good advice based on her experience first time round: 'A lesson I have had is how ill my little one has been since starting nursery. I naively thought that a couple of visits would give her some immunity but that hasn't been the case. That meant that I missed a lot of work just as I returned, which was an uncomfortable situation. I think if I ever go for baby number two, I'd put him or her in nursery for at least two to three days a week at least a month before I returned to work; that way there's a better chance of the baby getting some immunity.'

## Mums' Top Tips

❀ 'When your little one is ill ... forget about your work; you are doing your main job of being a mother and doing a great job at it!' **Maxi**

❀ 'Jack's nursery flooded recently so I had to have two days off work. They called me in to advise me that since coming back to work I have had three occasions off due to having to look after my son. I advised them that I couldn't have done anything about it as I had no one else to look after him. They told me I had to get an "emergency plan" in case this happens again ... I told them that they'd kept me employed with the knowledge that I had a child! I don't think it went down too well but, still, if Jack is ill my main concern is for Jack, not for work.' **Clare**

## Being a stay-at-home mum

Many women face the dilemma of whether to go back to work. Deciding to stay at home and be a full-time mum isn't an easy decision either. I liked Louise's take on this: 'I think the key is to commit to whatever it is that you choose. I have friends who are full-time mums and effectively they approach it with the same discipline as they would a career. They absolutely make the best of it, work at it, seize every moment of it and ultimately make it work for them.' Charlie felt that one of the biggest challenges of being a stay-at-home mum was the loss of independence. Relying on someone else to provide for you is an adjustment if you've been used to having your own income. Talk this over with your partner. Decide what works for you – it might be that you have an allowance so that you feel that you have some independent money, or maybe, like some women, you actually control the joint account. Clare says that once a month she has the day off and goes shopping for the day. She meets a friend for lunch, and finds that it does her husband good to spend the day on his own with the kids.

## Mums' Top Tips

❀ 'If you are finding it hard to juggle everything (and can afford a little assistance), think hard about what you need help with. Do you want someone to look after the children while you clean the house, or someone to clean the house while you have fun with your little ones? I chose the cleaner!' **Kate**

❀ 'I found it hard in the early days, and needed to have a purpose every day – even if it was just going for a walk around the block. But over time I built up a great circle of friends and things got much easier. A good way to find new friends (once your toddler starts pre-school) is to join the committee. They are always crying out for members and it's a great way to meet other mums; even if you don't find your "new best friend", you will always find people to chat to.' **Claire**

❀ 'I joined a gym and I exercise regularly. I also keep a keen interest in the news, current affairs and technology so when my hubby comes home I can talk to someone about something other than the price of nappies and what my little one has done that day.' **Charlie**

❀ 'Because you are at home all day, make time to meet friends in the evening. The day will be easier if you have something to look forward to, and you will feel like an adult again – put on some lipstick, add perfume and a pair of high heels and shrug off the baby-blues. After a glass of wine and a laugh with girlfriends you will actually look forward to seeing your sleeping babes again.' **Kate**

❀ 'I would never say that being a stay-at-home mum is easy, but I've never found it stressful in the way my job was stressful. Yes, my son is all-consuming and exhausting from time to time, but toddlers are just completely joyous. And they will never threaten to take you to an employment tribunal, thank goodness!' **Kay**

❀ 'It gets better, especially when they start walking, talking and generally being silly. My daughter has me in fits of laughter for the most part.' **Susan**

❀ 'I enjoyed my job, but sometimes you just get bogged down in the minutiae of other people: life with a toddler is uncomplicated, straightforward and utterly joyous.' **Becky**

❀ 'Having spent the first few years at home with my children, at least I know that whatever hang-ups they may have later in life they have got them from me!' **Kate**

❀ 'If you choose to stay at home rather than going back to work, try to get some form of childcare once or twice a week – even if it's just the local crèche for a couple of hours. It gives you some time off and lets your little one get used to being with other people.' **Laura**

❀ 'It really is worth inviting other mums to your house. I found out later that most other first-time mums felt in need of company, just as I did. It's just that we all put on a brave front when we don't know each other well.' **Natasha**

❀ 'The days are always so busy, so I have an objective of always spending some one-to-one time every day just playing with the children, even if it's only 15 minutes. That way, I don't feel like I'm just running round doing housework and cooking, etc. I get time to enjoy the girls – it's the rewarding side of motherhood so shouldn't be neglected!' **Jillian**

❀ 'If you follow a routine with your children, then you can plan your own day effectively and multi-task much better, as you know when they will sleep, need to be fed and need entertaining. I plan my food menu for the coming week on a Sunday night. While my baby has his lunchtime nap, my toddler and I cook and prepare dinner together and I find he eats much better if he's had a hand in the preparation. Then we sit together and have some special time, reading books and doing puzzles. The afternoon is then spent doing an activity or going for a long walk to the park, or on an outing. I find if I plan and organise the outings at the start of the week, I am better prepared on the day and not as stressed getting everyone out and into the car.' **Kim**

### CLB Mums' Top 10 Best Tips ... for Being a Stay-at-home Mum

1. Avoid housework as much as possible!

2. Spend lots of time with other mums who have babies the same age.

3. Remember that it does get easier. When it does, you'll find you've forgotten quite how hard it was and have another one!

4. Plan your time just like you would if you were working. Plan nice things too, so you have things to look forward to when you're doing the boring stuff.

5. Have lunch with the girls; it does require a bit of multi-tasking, but not only does it save time, it also makes the whole feeding thing much more pleasant and family-like especially if, like me, you hate eating alone!

6. Get showered and dressed before dealing with the family. It's a nice quiet start to the day when you get time to think about the day ahead and work yourself slowly into action.

7. Involve the children as early as possible in household chores. It turns chores into fun for everyone and you get to spend time with the children while still getting things done.

8. Have a weekly routine, so that, for example, you know you always go to your fitness class on Monday morning, toddler gym on Wednesday afternoon, the weekly shop on Friday. That way, you begin to have a structure, around which you can add on the fun stuff – meet friends, go to the park, have coffee in town and so on.

9. Get wireless broadband and a laptop so you can stay in touch with people while keeping an eye on your little one.

10. It's easy to begin to feel inferior if friends are talking about high-powered jobs, but remember that you are doing the most important job of all. It can be hard at parties when people ask, 'What do you do?' but the best answer (if you've got the nerve!) is, 'Anything I like, what do you do?'

## Getting out of the house

If you're a stay-at-home mum, it's crucial that you spend time outside of the house. This is good for both you and your baby. As well as visiting friends and relatives and outings to the park, look for local groups you can attend. There's also no reason why you can't enjoy some activities without your baby, as CLB mum Kate found out: 'One of the best things I did was to take my twins to the crèche at my local leisure centre as soon as they would have them (about six weeks), so that I could do an exercise class. This proved a lifesaver – having a whole hour where I focused on nothing but the exercise kept me sane, *and* made me feel good about myself. And because I did it regularly, right from when they were tiny, I never had a problem with the twins being upset at being left.'

### Mums' Top Tips

* 'Be brave about inviting children and mums for coffee and then they'll return the favour. I found this hard to begin with – a bit like being back at school and making friends again.' **Louise**

* 'Baby and toddler groups are an absolute godsend – an opportunity to meet other parents and carers. They can also act as a good counselling session as well as keeping your little one entertained. Also invest in a good buggy

that can be used either for jogging or walking and embrace all weathers. There's something very refreshing about walking in the rain with your little one all wrapped up in the buggy.' **Charlie**

- 'Make sure you do some things that are for you and you alone. On the days when it's just me and the baby, I make sure we go swimming, for a walk or to a local playgroup. I will talk to anyone when I'm out and about, and having a baby in the pram is always good for starting a conversation.' **Kate**

- 'I make sure I get out of the house every day, even if it's just to the post office. It blows the cobwebs away and I always find the children easier to deal with when they've been out. Also plan a nice outing regularly – I do it once a week. There are always so many excuses not to do the non-essential things and it can be a big effort getting everyone ready and fitting it in between feeding, sleeping and all the rest, but it is really the fun side of motherhood and makes me feel good about being a stay-at-home mum.' **Jillian**

## Mum-to-Mum: *Dealing with criticism*

### Query

*'My baby is four months old now and a few people have started asking me when I intend going back to work. The majority of*

*women I know seem to think that choosing not to work is some sort of "cop out". People have said things to me like: "Oh, I couldn't not work, I think my brain would rot," "Don't you need to be someone other than 'Mummy'?" and "Your relationship with your husband will suffer as he won't see you as attractive anymore." I think, maybe, 10–15 years ago, mothers who chose to go to work were stigmatised as being "bad mothers". Now, I'm being made to feel that I'm selling the sisterhood short by wanting to be at home for the first few years of my kids' lives. What have others found? Am I being naive to think that I can take a career break, be with my kids (almost) full-time and still stay sane?'* **Laura**

## Answers

'Snap. Before I had my baby, I was a doctor training to be a surgeon. There is absolutely no way that I could have a vaguely successful surgical career and see my baby as regularly as I'd like. The comments I have received – all that wasted training, etc. One grandmother at a mother and baby group accused me of wasting her taxes! People just don't hold back with their opinions and seem to feel perfectly at liberty to interfere with your decisions. Our current set-up suits our family perfectly and our daughter is thriving. I'm so sorry for wasting the tax money of anyone reading this!' **Emma**

'You can't win! I'm the opposite – as an engineering manager, I earn twice my partner's salary and couldn't afford not to go back to work. I constantly find myself justifying not being there all the time. I hone in on all the newspaper articles saying that working mums are damaging their children by not being there for them. You have to do what you feel is best. I personally feel that children should be brought up and cared for by their parents. Unfortunately, that is not always the ideal situation for all concerned so you compromise.' **Beth**

'I get so fed up with people saying, "Don't you get bored?" and "What do you do all day?" I did go back to work after I had my first and hated it. I missed her terribly and found I couldn't give 100 per cent to my job so I gave it up to spend my time with her. It suits our circumstances perfectly and, yes, I do sometimes wish I worked but at the end of the day my children are only small once. My brain isn't rotting (to the best of my knowledge!) and my relationship with my husband is not suffering.' **Rose**

'The important thing is that you are happy with your decision. I think mums should be supported in their decisions. We seem to have become such an intolerant society and, worst of all, presume that people aren't making the "right" decision – thus need to be told. Who do these people think they are?' **Cathy**

'Your brain going to mush? What rubbish. My brain seems to work much better now as I think up new ways to amuse my son, fathom out the logistics of going out anywhere, plan my day so I can get as much done as possible, and that's before he's talking and I have to think up more new ways to amuse him and answer the dreaded "Why?" questions. My advice ... tell them all to wind their necks in and mind their own business. It's your life and if they think you are selling out for an easy life then let them walk a day in your shoes and see how they get on then.' **Debbie**

'To all you stay-at-home mums, I completely and utterly take my hat off to you. I find looking after two kids the most rewarding, frustrating and generally bone-wearying thing ever. I am still on maternity leave but am already fighting the compulsion to go back to work. I love my kids but I also love my job. A lot of my friends are stay-at-home mums and they think that I'm superwoman for going back to work, looking after kids, etc. but honestly I think it's the other way round. Work gives me the chance to have "me-time" and feel like someone other than Mummy.' **Maria**

'When I realised that there was no way that I wanted to go back to a boring, dead-end job that I didn't like, and didn't want to leave my baby, I spent months working out what I could do instead. That is when I came up with my new business idea. Everyone, especially my mum, challenged my foolish idea – how do I know I can earn enough? Well, I don't, but if I don't try I'll never know! What a waste of all of those years of study – er, no. Actually the training for a business accountant will stand me in good stead for running my own business. All of my friends think my brain will rot, but to be honest it rotted in my previous job! It is the best decision I have ever made. I can already say that, even though I haven't gone live yet. It is very hard work – every time the baby sleeps, I work, but at least I'm not doing a job I hate, and I get to spend every day with my little one.' **Wendy**

'It took me ages to stop immediately referring to what I "used" to do when I met new people. I was so insecure that they would think of me as "just" a stay-at-home mum. I was also quite shocked that my female peers were the ones with the most catty comments. Then one day it really hit me that I am so very lucky. I have a choice as to whether I stay at home or go out to work, a husband who has always supported my decision – that in itself is such a blessing.' **Rozanna**

'There is nothing more annoying for mums to read every day than about how we damage our kids and the comments from other people on what they think is best. Don't listen to anyone and do what feels right for you.' **Leanne**

'I am a stay-at-home-mum and a proud one too! And I will be until we're done having babies and they are all a little older. I had only just started working after completing a MSc degree when I fell pregnant and I now have a dream of being a midwife sometime in the future – absolutely nothing to do with what I'm already qualified to do, and I am quite content to wait. And I don't feel guilty or like a cop-out.'

**Gina says:** Although it's difficult, try to focus on what's right for you and ignore those who comment and criticise. If you're in any doubt about whether you're still doing 'a good job', listen to what Kim had to say: 'The challenges I face every day as a mother, both physically and emotionally, are not for the faint-hearted and have broadened my horizons immeasurably. I love my job, I'm just not paid! I, too, must add that I feel very blessed that I have a husband who supports me and wants me at home with the kids, and who places no importance on the material things that an extra salary could generate. My belief is that we must do what our hearts tell us to do and do it with confidence and conviction, whether that's working or staying at home.'

And there was some great advice from Rozanna: 'Accept that every choice has its pros and cons – make the best of the situation that you are in. Take pride in yourself and what you do and set goals for yourself. Stop justifying your decision. When you really know you have made the right choice for yourself and your family, you can be at peace. At the end of the day, stay-at-home mums and working mums all share the same joys, frustrations, fears and "Am I doing things right?" guilt. Our babies love us whatever our choice; we should learn to do the same.'

## Summary – points to remember

### Returning to work

- If you are going back to work purely for financial reasons, then make the most of this. Think of ways you and your family will benefit from this extra money, such as enjoying family days out together.

- If you can't bear to leave your little one, discuss with your partner ways in which you can change your lifestyle so that you are able to spend more time at home.

- Make the most of whatever work offers – be it the opportunity to wear smart clothes, time to have a coffee on your own, stimulating adult conversation or 20 minutes to read a book on the train home.

- Be organised. If you need to leave the house early in the morning, prepare the evening before, with everything you and your little one need for the day.

- Try not to worry – it will take time for you and your baby to settle into your new daily routines, but I assure you that very soon it will all run like clockwork.

- Involve your partner. Perhaps you can share the childcare, or take turns dropping off and picking up from nursery. And don't forget that you both need time to yourselves too.

### Childcare

- Research nurseries before the birth of your baby. The good ones become oversubscribed – and you will have little time to look once you are caring for your little one.

- Ask friends which nurseries and childminders they are happy with. A personal recommendation is often worth as much as a good Ofsted report.

- Go with your instinct. Don't ignore any nagging doubts you may have about a nursery or childminder.

# 6

# Extending the Family

Your tiny newborn is growing up and has developed into a settled baby who sleeps and eats well. Or perhaps you have a happy, chatty toddler and life seems so much simpler now that he can talk. Around this time, you and your partner might be considering how lovely it would be to have a baby brother or sister for your growing child. This can be a daunting prospect, however. You have just got your little one sleeping through the night and the thought of having to cope with broken nights' sleep again can be enough to prevent you embarking on conceiving another child. Diana speaks for many parents at this time, saying, 'In our hearts we both know we want another baby, but in the meantime we are both scared when we think about the sacrifices we will have to make.'

Fortunately, this feeling doesn't usually last long and most parents decide those sacrifices are worth making – as illustrated by families everywhere, including our many members who have gone on to have their second, third or even fourth child. In this chapter, many have delightful stories to share and encourage you to grow your family.

So, now you're convinced you'd like another child, but what age gap should you leave between your children? There are as many opinions as there are possibilities, so whatever you aim for, you will find someone whose experience you can share. Nature, of course, has the final say, so my main advice is to relax and enjoy this precious time with the little ones you already have – and appreciate that there are benefits to all age gaps.

If you are currently expecting your second child, then you are quite possibly experiencing the tiredness commonly associated with pregnancy, which is exacerbated by the need to care for your busy toddler or older child. This exhaustion can lead to real doubts concerning your ability to cope with another child, particularly if child number one is going through a challenging stage. To ensure a harmonious larger family, I have gathered masses of tips and strategies, which will allay any concerns as well as providing practical advice on coping with the daily challenges that obviously arise. The first few weeks with a toddler and baby are bound to be hard, as everyone re-adjusts to the new family dynamics and demands of a tiny baby. But, in time, the good days will swiftly outnumber the less successful ones and your baby's routine will soon fall into place and fit in with your family life. Above all, don't be too hard on yourself, particularly in the early days. Judi, mother of a baby and a toddler, was delighted with the results of following this principle: 'I will always remember my daughter's first year as one filled with cuddles, laughter and a much less stressed-out Mummy, which in turn has made two very laid-back, affectionate, happy little girls.' What more could a mother ask for?

And once you have two children, for some people the question of a third arises. The implications of this are more far-reaching, as Julia points out: 'Should I take such a risk? Financially it would be hard with a third – we would have to change car, introduce bedroom-sharing or move house, and what about school fees if we wish to give them private education?' It's important to weigh up the emotional cost as well as the practicalities. Julia continues: 'I've heard about Middle Child Syndrome and would hate to reduce the quality of life my second child has. Is two children a good number to stick at given I've only got two knees to be sat upon and can only hug two people at once? As an only child of only children I was always lonely and wonder if this is why I wish to rebel and have a larger family? Or is it those hormones again?!' The overall message from our mothers of three, amidst the hugely positive and supportive advice, is that although life is very busy, it's wonderful and they wouldn't change it – even if number three appeared somewhat unexpectedly or earlier than anticipated!

Whatever the size of your family, and whatever number of children you end up with, there is heaps of thoughtful and sensible advice here to guide you through the early days. Do try to make sure you take the time to enjoy all your children, and appreciate the different characteristics and individual gifts that they contribute to your contented family.

# Wanting another child

One of the main concerns for many parents is how another baby will affect the children they already have, and ensuring they get the right age gap between children. Christine says: 'I think if the age gap is very small between the first and second child, say less than 18 months, then the elder child's sense of identity is not established and so not knocked off kilter by the arrival of a new baby. The same is true when the age gap is much larger, say five years. You don't need to worry about any of this when thinking of a third or subsequent child – only the first-born has the exclusive attention of his parents and so is most unsettled when it is denied him.'

## Mums' Top Tips

❀ 'I would not change it for the world. When the day feels like it has been the hardest day ever, so much to do and nobody is happy ... well I learn through it. I've changed and grown through the challenges and demands.' **Anna**

❀ 'I love watching my three children interact; they have so much fun playing together. The eldest is such a "mum" to the other two. She tells them what they can and can't do and tells them off if they are "naughty". I think it is just a matter of time before my three realise that they outnumber us! Then we can only hope they are well-disciplined enough not to run off when we take them out.' **Elizabeth**

❁ 'After having twins, I always knew that I wanted another child – I wanted to experience what everyone else had, a singleton! And when my daughter arrived two-and-a-half years after my boys, it was an utter joy and a revelation. Having only one baby to look after seemed so easy after having twins – only one little one to feed, change, bathe, and no one crying while waiting for attention. To any mother of twins, I would highly recommend having another. I enjoyed every moment of my daughter's baby days.' **Kate**

❁ 'The worst thing you can do is to put any kind of pressure on yourself to conceive at this time or that. Your body doesn't respond well to blackmail.' **Charlotte**

❁ 'Don't wait too long if you want number three – a friend of mine has waited and now there is a five-year gap between the second and third and she's finding that hard, as her oldest two children seem a bit resentful.' **Alice**

❁ 'We have a large, deliberate gap of nearly six years between our two. Neither of us felt that we could cope looking after two very small children. It has been great that our eldest can do everything for herself, and has totally different needs to a small baby. There's also no jealousy there, because she just enjoys having a baby sister to show off to her school friends. We had so many comments from people asking when we were going to have our "next" one – it only stopped about a year before our second baby was conceived! It's a good idea to get advice from people, but make sure that the decision you make is absolutely the right one for you both, and make sure that you don't feel pressured into one thing or another.' **Sarah**

❀ 'Don't think about the gap and just enjoy trying for that baby! If your husband is anything like mine, he will relish having a small window between babies when you can make the most of doing something that just involves the two of you!' **Joanna**

## ◼ Mum-to-Mum: *Small age gap*

### Query

*'My baby is nine months old and I'm starting to think about baby number two. My husband and I always thought we'd like at least three years in between, but now I'm wondering about having them much closer than that. I'd love to hear from any mums with children close together.'* **Rebecca**

## Answers

'We have a two-year age gap between ours, so we have two in nappies, and my eldest still needs help feeding and dressing. She speaks well but of course is still learning to communicate so that can be hard sometimes. On the positive side, I think it's because she's so young that she coped really well with the arrival of her baby brother. I don't think she can remember a time now when he wasn't around. I get lots of time with her when the baby is in bed and they both nap at lunchtime so give me an hour off! It is really exhausting and so much harder than one, but I wouldn't change a thing.' **Katie**

'My two children are 16 months apart. The hardest thing was trying to fit two routines into a day, while not disturbing the older child's existing routine and interests. It has taken me three months to feel "normal" again. However, I wouldn't have it any other way. My daughter adores her little brother and he watches her and smiles away as she is playing. It's so cute to see. Also when they are a little older, they will be great friends (and enemies!) and be into the same things together.' **Lari**

'There are 15 months between mine and they are now aged five and four. As babies, it was really hard, and made even harder by the fact that we have no family around us. I printed out both of the kids' routines and stuck them to the fridge as memory loss coupled with sleep deprivation sent me slightly loopy! For the last 12 to 18 months it has been really wonderful watching the kids interact, have their own conversations and be into similar things. They both absolutely dote on each other and look out for each other.' **Kady**

'My son was 13 months old when my daughter was born. It was hell at the beginning, but now they're best of friends. It was almost like having twins – they dropped their naps at the same time and I potty-trained them together. We can't remember what life was like without her and they get on brilliantly.' **Mary**

'I think it depends on your situation. We don't have any help and both work, which means we juggle the care of the children between us. I think if you are lucky enough to have help, it would make it easier.' **Kelly**

'I have 14 months between my boys, and they are now aged seven and six. Our first-born was terribly jealous, since he was still a baby himself when his brother arrived. He was also slow to walk, so for about six months I had two babies needing to be carried – one newborn, the other 14 months! It was exhausting. If it wasn't for the CLB routines, I suspect my husband and I would never have contemplated a third, but I am expecting a little girl in the spring – so in time I'll be able to tell you how the bigger gap works!' **Fifi**

'I know we gave this lots of thought, but then once we had decided on a two-year gap, it took me 18 months to get pregnant so we ended up with nearer three. So my advice is don't try to plan these things too rigorously or you may put yourself through heartache. I was so hung up on having my second child and my inability to conceive that I stopped enjoying what I had – a gorgeous little toddler with bags of energy.' **Elisabeth**

**Gina says:** There is plenty of good advice from the CLB mums. In my experience it is always more difficult when the toddler is aged 18 months to two years, probably because this is a period when he is learning many new skills. Talking, potty-training and getting dressed are major hurdles in a toddler's life. A mother coping with a new baby can often find it difficult to remain patient when teaching these new things, and the toddler quickly picks up on the mother's tension. With this age gap, getting the baby into a routine is paramount, as it will mean you have the time needed to help your toddler cope with learning the different skills.

One view I found interesting was that of natural nutritionist Vardit Kohn, who says, 'Chinese medicine says it is best to wait a minimum of two years between the birth of a baby and the next pregnancy. This advice is based on the belief that pregnancy, breastfeeding and childcare take a big toll on your body and two years gives you time to replenish.'

Like so many decisions we make, there are pros and cons to having a small age gap between children. Here CLB mum Laura sums them up for us based on her own experiences:

**Pros**

- It gets the baby stage out of the way ... for me that's a definite plus, as now, just over a year since having my second, they are both getting to the stage of being able to interact, and becoming more independent. However, if you love the early months then obviously this wouldn't be a good thing, as you'd want more time focusing solely on your young baby.

- They have a close relationship.

- My daughter was young enough that I wasn't even contemplating things like potty-training but old enough to be self-feeding. By the time she was ready for potty-training, she'd already totally adjusted to the baby. I know mums who have had a terrible time with their three-year-old weeing on the floor whenever mum feeds the baby. I think a certain amount of 'regression' is to be expected and, I suppose, the smaller the gap, the less the older one has to regress towards, if that makes sense!

**Cons**

- The first six months were incredibly hard, but then again maybe I would have felt that whatever the age gap.

- Not having time to totally devote to my eldest when she was learning lots of new skills, like dressing, language, etc. I feel a bit bad for her that I was so distracted and tired for so much of her major developmental stages. Oh well, something else to feel guilty about!

## ■ Mum-to-Mum: *Loving a second child*

### Query

*'Will I bond as easily with my second child, despite having so little time to think about him or her?'* **Gwennie**

### Answers

'Of course you will. It is one of the most amazing aspects of motherhood. You'll fall in love just as deeply and irrevocably as you did with number one!' **Louisa**

'I worried about loving the second child with the same depth. I couldn't believe I could love anyone or anything as much as I did my son. But when my little girl arrived, I couldn't believe I had ever doubted that I would feel as strongly. She is so beautiful and gorgeous, and I am finding it all so much easier than I did the first time around.' **Carrie**

**Gina says:** These fears are very normal. As a new mum, you give so much to your first baby that you can't possibly imagine having any love, let alone energy, left for the second. But don't underestimate the power of those maternal feelings that will naturally kick in once you see your precious second child.

## Benefits of having another child

The prospect of having another baby, whether you have one, two or three already, can be daunting, but there are many benefits. Here are the CLB mums' experiences:

### Mums' Top Tips

✿ 'Having to deal with a baby has taught my six-year-old and four-year-old consideration for others.' **Claire**

✿ 'I love family life so much. We have a lot to give still and I want to get more out of the experience of being a parent.' **Dawn**

✿ 'Think ahead to when your children are adults – wouldn't it be great for them to have siblings. Maybe not a deal-maker, but worth a thought!' **Kate**

✿ 'The good thing about second children is that we just don't have the time to rock them to sleep and worry about them, which means that they learn to fall asleep themselves much sooner. You will be a much more confident mum the second time around; the first ones we make lots of mistakes with, but they survive.' **Elizabeth**

✿ 'We were all walking in the woods together when my toddler got tired. I watched in amazement as my eight-year-old bent down and picked her up in a piggyback without a murmur. She's helped make the boys more patient and considerate. And I have consciously enjoyed her in a way I didn't always the first two times.' **Wendy**

✿ 'My friend Sarah is one of six, and she speaks very fondly of her own childhood. She says that the children brought each other up and were always there for each other, and parental influence was reduced – probably because there was less time for so much individual attention. She certainly hasn't suffered, and all the children felt equally loved and important.' **Kate**

## ■ Mum-to-Mum: *Feeling broody*

### Query

*'I'm so happy having two children and the reality of a third really doesn't appeal to me at all but I can't get my head round the fact that my baby days are over. My youngest is almost walking, and pretty much self-feeding too, and it makes me feel*

*totally down that there'll be no more feeling the baby kick, no more labour, no more sleepy night-feeds, no more new baby smells, no more tiny fingers and toes. What's happening to me? I don't even really like the baby stage!'* Laura

## Answers

'I think we women are weird creatures! I have this unusual attraction to labour and being pregnant again, and have spent the last few days thinking, "Oh no, they're not babies any more!" And they are only 21 months and five months old! I don't think we'll have any more, as we have got to consider our quality of life. Perhaps if we had support from extended family that might make a difference. A few of my friends have said that once they hit 40, the real broody stage passed! That's what I'm hoping anyway.' Catriona

'I don't like pregnancy as I was very sick, but the thought of never seeing a positive pregnancy test again ... and that over-whelming feeling of excitement. I just can't imagine it. Both mine have been great babies too. Of course it's hard work and some days I can't cope but the thought of not doing it again fills me with despair!' Claire

'My husband made me write a pros-and-cons list. Needless to say we are sticking with two ...' Kady

'My friend who has three children says it's getting harder as they get older as they need more support, not less. Now she spends her evenings driving them about to different groups, etc. She reckons she and her husband have even less time and energy for each other now than they did when they had babies. A cautionary tale for all broody women.' **Laura**

'I remember complaining when my little one was about three months old and just didn't sleep and someone at work said wait until he's taking GCSEs – then you'll know what hard work is! Maybe that thought is an effective form of birth control! Remember, one day we might all be grand-parents and then we'll get the baby love but also be able to hand them back and sleep!' **Sophie**

'I'm only going to have two, and although my son is only 11 weeks, I'm already feeling odd about the fact that these are my last baby days. I walk round the house holding him and just loving his babyness.' **Susie**

'I'm pregnant with my third and probably my last, and I'm already feeling broody! My hubby said the other day that he would book in for the snip. I jumped and said "No, not yet!"' **Amy**

**Gina says:** Feelings of broodiness are completely normal but you will come to terms with them in time. Maybe you can get your baby 'fix' with friends' or relatives' newborns? It can help to focus on the wonderful next stage in your children's development, which can be equally rewarding. Kady says: 'My children are now going to lots of different groups, such as dancing and swimming, and they get invited to tea parties. And if I want more kids, I always have additional ones at my house! I can see a new stage in my little ones' lives that make nappies, night-feeds and getting stressed over breastfeeding all seem like a distant but happy memory.'

## Coping with another child

If you were running a business, you'd begin with a business plan. You would map out in advance specific objectives and exactly what you wanted to achieve. These might be challenging but they would be realistic. It's no different running a home and taking care of children. Each day you have specific chores and tasks you have to do – they might seem mundane in comparison, but shopping, cooking nutritious meals, playing with your kids and keeping everyone happy is probably the most important job you'll ever do, even if it doesn't always feel that way! Understanding and recognising what is possible, and what isn't, is the key to a happy household.

Having more than one baby will inevitably put a strain on your relationship and it's even more important to keep the lines of communication open. Sit down with your partner and be honest about how you feel and the support you need; listen to what he has to say too. CLB mum Maria says, 'Don't be a martyr – if something needs to be said, say it. Don't bottle it up. Often just the process of sharing a problem can help you feel a lot better. Resentment easily builds up when communication is poor, especially when fuelled by the exhaustion of disrupted nights.'

Prioritise, delegate or just leave some of the tasks for another day. There will always be something else to be done, just remember your perspective and set aside time for the children, your partner and yourself. Of course you need to be realistic about the time that you do have, but even 15 minutes doing something really enjoyable can give you energy and enthusiasm for the day.

CLB mum Briony says that as your children get older, you should encourage them to entertain themselves and play with each other. 'You'll create a rod for your own back if they don't learn to spend at least part of every day amusing themselves. Learn to let them be and only intervene if a situation gets dangerous or out of control. Love them, play with them and above all else make time to enjoy them. The childhood years fly by so fast, before you know it they'll be teenagers and you'll have a whole new set of problems to worry about!'

## Mums' Top Tips

✿ 'Staggered bedtimes mean that each child gets some one-to-one time at the end of the day so goes to bed feeling relaxed. Mornings are also staggered. Bathtime and meal-times are all together so no cooking several meals, no running and emptying several baths. It's all done together, which the boys love, and it saves me time and energy. My boys are great eaters and I believe this is because we have always eaten the same foods and at the same time. No room for fussiness in a busy house like this!' **Kelly**

✿ 'Recognise that perfection is impossible. Your house needn't look like a show home – your children won't remember their home as being spotless, only that their mum was always too busy doing housework to play with them and they got into trouble when they made a mess.' **Briony**

✿ 'Stick to the routines, and believe in the routines – then even in the first few weeks, when you will be tired, you will know that you will get there in the end. Do what you need to in the early days. There have been lots of times when I have put a DVD on for my toddler while I was seeing to the baby. I know it's not the ideal thing to do, but such distractions do have a time and a place in the early days when you are struggling through!' **Ange**

❀ 'Remind yourself that we're the stronger sex and that's why we have them in the first place – and, yes, you can do this!' **Sallerina**

❀ 'Leave the car at home and walk, walk, walk. It's an effective, realistic way of keeping fit and it involves the children: we get a good chance to chat, we sing, and the baby loves it, of course. I think it's a stress-reducer, too.' **Jillian**

❀ 'When the weather is bad and we're all going a little stir-crazy in the house, I go for a drive with my toddler and baby. We sing along to the CD and the toddler and I played spot the deer, baby, cyclist, etc. and the baby is content to sit in the car looking out the window and listening to the CD.' **Judi**

❀ 'In very busy work times I have tried to do practically nothing outside just being at home, taking time to catch up on things for myself and time with the children. Adding more children to the family unit has required me to make more lists and plan more carefully so that I know that I am remembering to take care of things for each child.' **Dani**

❀ 'I have found it important to try to make time for each of my children individually at some point during the weekend.' **Jen**

❀ 'Take all the help you are offered and include grandparents
in babysitting if you can. I am on my own all day from 8am
to 8pm and it's difficult but I am used to it. Make sure your
bedtime routine is very organised, and then at least you
know you will get a break at the end of the day. Batch-
cook and get your partner to help with that!' **Claire**

## ■ Mum-to-Mum: *Three under three*

### Query

*'I found out last week that I am pregnant, which means I will
have three children aged under three. Does anyone have any
advice for dealing with this?'* **Amy**

### Answers

'I always plan everything and know what I am doing each
day. My fridge is covered in lists! Work on any sleeping issues
now before the baby arrives. I had to do some controlled
crying with my one-year-old before the baby arrived to
ensure he was sleeping through. It worked well and meant I
was only dealing with one child waking each night. Each
child has a toy box. I bring a selection down each evening for
the next day. It's easier to keep tidy and means the kids are
not overwhelmed by too many. I also find it handy to have a
supply of nappies and wipes both up- and downstairs, and I
keep a fully packed changing bag in the car. I re-stock it after

each outing and put it back in the boot – then if I need to dash out it's fine. I am sure you will find it less daunting than everyone else imagines. It is challenging sometimes but I love it.' **Kelly**

'The more children you have, the more stuff you have. The Argos toy storage system is great. The boxes can be labelled and easily pulled in and out by the children, and the toys moved to another room as required. It is also a great height for them to use as another play surface. I can't recommend something like this strongly enough. Loads of my friends have bought one.' **Claire**

'I recommend getting the sleeping issues sorted nice and early. I definitely wouldn't have the two older ones sharing until the sleeping is resolved. Don't worry too much about how hard it might be; it is very rewarding and lots of fun really (once they are sleeping through the night).' **Liz**

'I still get lots of stares at the shops and people stop us to say how hard it must be with three kids so young. I have loved watching my three grow up together; they enjoy all the same things because they are so close in age.' **Elizabeth**

**Gina says:** As you know, I'm a great believer in routines and they are essential when you're dealing with three children under three. It's also important to have a good support network. If you don't have family nearby, look to other mums for advice. Claire says, 'The CLB website is great. You often can't see the wood for the trees yourself and need a hand figuring things out, which of course the CLB mums help you do!'

## ▪ Mum-to-Mum: *Preparing your toddler for a baby*

### Query

*'My baby will be 15 months old when his little brother or sister arrives. I'd love some insight into what to expect. Some people say they are too young to get jealous, others say they are even more jealous because they just don't understand.'* **Susie**

### Answers

'We tried to explain to my toddler that Mummy had a baby sister growing in her tummy and we would ask him, "Where is the new baby?" and he would touch my tummy. I'm not sure how much he understood, though! I've found that giving my toddler the extra attention when the baby has her morning nap works wonders. Also, I usually resort to CBeebies when breastfeeding as it takes a while. I did have one scary moment, which I can now laugh about, when the baby projectile-vomited all over the sofa and my toddler found it great fun to rub his hands in it! The first few weeks he was not interested at all in his new sister. If we asked him to give her a kiss he would literally cringe. This last week he has started giving her kisses of his own accord, which is sweet!' **Sophie**

'My toddler showed no interest or real understanding of me being pregnant and was not really interested when the baby was born. It's only now, almost eight months down the line, that he seems to enjoy his brother. I also encouraged him to help me with things like bathtime and nappy changes. We just went with the flow and acted on his reactions to the new baby.' **Kelly**

'We taught our toddler very early on to be "gentle" with the cats, and so when the baby came, it was easy to teach him to be gentle with her. I reckon he thought she was a cat for the first three months!' **Amy**

'Other than patting my fat tummy (which she thought was hilarious), we said "baby" a lot and showed our toddler pictures of babies. One thing I wasn't prepared for was how torn you feel between looking after your new baby, which is so time-consuming, and paying enough attention to your other child. It's physically impossible in some instances, so it's important to have other people to help if you can, just for the first few months when it's so hard for you.' **Tracy**

'No one amuses a little baby like a toddler does and it really puts a huge smile on your face. Also, toddlers even from an earlyish age love the idea of helping out and my daughter has become a little bit of a slave for me as she seems to enjoy it and I figure she won't enjoy it for long so I use her while I can!' **Serena**

---

### CLB Mums' Top 10 Best Ways ... to Prepare Your Toddler for Baby's Arrival

1. Read 'Mummy's having a baby' type board books every night from about halfway through your pregnancy.

2. Buy a beanbag for your toddler to lie in while drinking his milk and listening to stories, so he will get used to not being in Mummy's lap at milk and storytime when you might need to feed the baby.

3. If possible, get your partner to take over the morning routine about two months prior to giving birth, so that your toddler is used to it.

4. Buy your toddler a special toy from the new baby.

5. Get your partner to text you when he's arrived at the hospital and, if possible, make sure the baby is in his cot at that time and not being breastfed. This way you can take the toddler to the baby and introduce them.

6. Give your toddler a bear or dolly to put to bed at the same time you put the baby to bed.

7.  Get your toddler involved – with passing you items when you're changing nappies; holding the peg basket when you're hanging out washing; letting him 'wash' the baby's toes in the bath!

8.  As the baby gets older, teach the toddler to find her another toy, when she is playing with something he wants, instead of snatching.

9.  Before the birth, we had my in-laws come up about two weeks prior, and got them to look after our toddler for short spells here and there, as they were going to look after him when I was in labour.

10. Teach your toddler 'eyes', 'nose', 'mouth', etc. ... so that he understands where not to poke his hands.

# Coping with a toddler and a baby

Having two children is difficult but when one is a toddler and one a baby it's arguably even more difficult. The answer – routine, routine, routine! The CLB mums say they don't know how they would have survived caring for a baby and a toddler at the same time if they hadn't followed a great routine with both of them. CLB mum Kim adds: 'Aside from a routine, it's important to make sure that each child gets some special time alone with you each day, as well as some time when you play with them both together. I think it's important for toddlers to see you actively play with your baby so that they, too, know how to play with him or her. I see my toddler copy my play with my baby when he thinks I'm not looking, so I always make a special emphasis on playing gently and fairly. I also find that when I make time to play with them on the floor for half an hour, they are much happier to entertain themselves for a short spell while I get a few chores done.'

If your toddler is active and not the type to sit still, try this: establish a ritual where the toddler has several little beds (painted boxes, with handmade blankets, etc.) to put his special toys to sleep. He can, in turn, give each toy a drink from their own special bottle or beaker before tucking them up and kissing them goodnight. Have a special toy in the baby's room that also has its own bed, so that when you take the baby through to settle him in his cot, your toddler can bring the special toy through and quietly tuck it up for the night. Another great tip came from Sallerina. She kept a 'special' box of toys for her toddler to play with while she fed the baby; he was only allowed the box at these times.

In the first three months with a newborn and a toddler, take life one day at a time, or even one hour, and get as much help as you can. Monique says, 'You soon realise that you cannot be in two places at once, no matter how much you would like to be and I'd rather accept that, than stress out about everything.' And Laura had these positive words: 'The good news is that, as they get older, the bad days soon get outnumbered by the good days – and you'll soon start to see your kids developing their own sibling relationship, which is gorgeous.'

## Mums' Top Tips

❀ 'Every good nursery has a written daily schedule, which means they know what they should be doing and when. They tend to factor in activities in short bursts, so that just at the time the children are losing interest in one thing, they move on to another. Do this at home – think of your day in terms of hourly (maximum) slots. This will also make it easier to give each child some individual attention exactly when they need it.' **Briony**

❀ 'Don't forget to listen. Listening to everyone, including the toddler, will help you all to offload and understand the strains being experienced.' **Maria**

❀ 'Don't feel guilty for having some alone time with the baby. Enjoy it, as they aren't wee babies for very long!' **Kady**

❀ 'You don't have to lose all of your old life – once you have got through the initial weeks of introducing the baby to the household and established a routine, there is no reason why you can't go back to some of your old activities. In fact, this sense of familiarity will prove reassuring for all and will introduce the baby to rituals that they will be part of from an early age. Maybe start going back to the café for Sunday brunch when your baby is napping. This can be an ideal time to focus on your toddler and give him your undivided attention.' **Maria**

✿ 'Breastfeeding number one was a great experience; I sat in front of the fire watching daytime TV and eating biscuits. Breastfeeding number two, I sat on the cold kitchen floor while trying to build blocks with a two-year-old who was intent on putting her finger up the baby's nose. I tried to keep everything running like clockwork, the house tidy and the routine strict until one day while I was potty-training one and weaning the other. I knew things had to change. I realised that I couldn't be so hard on myself. For the first year I spent much more time at home than I ever thought I would. I would see other mums when I wanted to rather than feeling I had to for the sake of my toddler. I would meet in the park for half an hour rather than a whole afternoon. My house may not be as spotless as it once was but it's fine. My toddler is not fluent in Mandarin, but she is potty-trained, nor can she recite Shakespeare but we have had a fabulous year!' **Judi**

✿ 'Second babies are a resilient lot, mostly because they have to entertain themselves such a lot of the time! But I think this is a good thing. Now, at a year, my baby plays really well by himself, and is happiest with a couple of books, or a car or two.' **Laura**

❀ 'One other thing I found to be a saviour was getting out our old playpen. I've put a soft blanket in it and filled it with the baby's toys, so it's a lovely place where he can lie, and my toddler can't get to him. It means that I can actually go to the loo by myself without having to drag Hugo along with me, in case he decides to lie on Sam!' **Rachel**

❀ 'I had my baby in the summer and found garden toys a great investment because it meant my boys spent loads of time in the garden happily playing while I concentrated on the baby.' **Claire**

## Putting your toddler first

You need to be aware of how the new baby will affect your toddler. Having been the apple of his parents' eye, there is now someone new who seems to get most of the attention. Time exclusively with your toddler is essential for him to feel reassured and secure in the new family.

A few minutes prior to settling the baby in the cot, make a point of using a very low, quiet voice to tell baby that he must be very quiet now as it is time to go in his cot so that you can read his big brother a very special story. Emphasise to the baby what a good boy his big brother is and how quiet he is. Of course this must all be done within earshot of the toddler!

Once the baby is settled in his cot, you can then take the toddler to his room and read him his special stories. You will have to be strict about how long you spend reading to him, otherwise a situation could arise where he will want just one more story and the bedtime settling begins to take longer and longer. I would suggest that you allow no longer than 15–20 minutes of reading.

## Mums' Top Tips

❀ 'I have tried to remember that what our toddler needs now is loads of reassurance, cuddles and attention, but also for as much as possible in her life to remain the same. I haven't relaxed any of our important rules (e.g. not being allowed to hit), but I have tried to make it easy for my toddler to be good and not asked too much of her. Whenever she does even the tiniest good thing, I give her loads of attention and praise.' **Sophie**

❀ 'Remember that your newborn won't mind being ignored between feeds – but your toddler will. It's hard to do, because you want to be with your new baby, but it really is okay to put the baby back in his crib after a feed and get back to the important task of interacting with your older child. I was able to do this as my second baby was a very easy, undemanding one, and it was great as I didn't feel guilty for not having time for my little boy.' **Kate**

❀ 'If your toddler asks for a cuddle while you are feeding your new baby, respond positively by saying, "We'll have a cuddle in a few minutes. If you come and sit next to me now, I can give you a kiss / read you a story / sing a song with you."' **Susie**

❀ 'I try to give my toddler 10 minutes' undivided attention a couple of times a day, where I just sit and allow her to boss me in child-led play! Storytime has become a bit longer at bedtime so that we get to have stories and cuddles.' **Catriona**

❀ 'Be prepared before a feed: line up two activities for your toddler, one for each half of the feed. For example, he could watch a short DVD for the first half. Once you have burped the baby, lay him down for a quick kick and give your toddler a cuddle and set him up with a new activity, such as doing a simple jigsaw. That way, he will remain engaged until the end of the feed instead of becoming bored with an activity that he has been doing for over half an hour.' **Susie**

❀ 'I make sure I spend at least one nap-time doing an activity with Grace.' **Rachel**

## ■ Mum-to-Mum: *Toddler trouble*

### Query

*'My three-year-old daughter has not been very good with the baby since he got on the move and started interfering with her stuff. She hits him, pushes him, shuts the door in his face, basically does what she can to make him cry. This morning was awful and ended with me putting her in her cot as she was hitting me too and I had had enough. She cried and cried, and said sorry. As I got her out, she said to me, "You can't have two specials, can you, Mummy?" I was so upset. Any ideas?'* Claire

### Answers

'I've found my relationship with my toddler has improved no end since we've started going out together on our own. I've really noticed that she's better behaved towards me since we started this, and she also even asks for me to take her to bed, which would never have happened six weeks ago. Maybe it's just coincidence, but I think we are getting on better.' Laura

'I read somewhere about creating a big "space" for the eldest one that the younger one isn't allowed to invade – for example, a big armchair. Or do things on the big table that the younger one can't reach. I think it's important that the elder one has somewhere where he can go for space. I would also get a bit cheesed off if I was working on something and suddenly chubby hands came in to interfere! Be reassured that it does get better.' **Anna**

'My daughter and I have our "Big Girls' Days Out", just the two of us. They're not as frequent as I'd like, but she really does enjoy them and feels special. I also enjoy them – after over two years of dragging two children everywhere, it's actually quite liberating and fun to just have to look after a three-year-old for a few hours.' **Alison**

## Summary – points to remember

- Whatever the age gap between your children, it will prove to be the right one for your family.

- A small age gap between babies may be hard work initially but will pay dividends in the future – you will have fewer issues with jealousy and your two little ones will be great companions.

- Families come in all sizes, and each family is the perfect fit.

- Organisation is key to looking after more than one child. Plan meals, have a weekly cleaning schedule and arrange regular activities.

- As the size of your family increases, don't expect your home to look like a show home. It's far more important to spend time playing with your little ones than keeping your home immaculate.

*In the early days of life with a new baby and a toddler*

- Remember that your CLB routines will guide you through the early days.

- Get as much help as you can – if friends offer to help, give them a task you would like done.

- Make time for your toddler when your baby is asleep.

- Make life easy for yourself and your toddler – don't embark on potty-training at this time, and avoid your toddler becoming over-tired.

- Accept that there will be days when all does not go according to plan. Learn from the tricky days.

# The Wonders of Motherhood

When it's all getting too much, turn to these wonderful and inspiring quotes that remind us just why it's so great to be a mum!

'Even on the toughest days, when she smiles at me it is the best feeling in the world.' **Fee**

'I loved my job to bits, but spending time with my daughter and seeing her doing new things every day is better than any career in the world for me.' **Lenita**

'It's like one big adventure waiting to see what will happen next.' **Joanne**

'I love it when my daughter points at Nigella Lawson on TV and says "Mummy" every time! What a compliment.' **Serena**

'My toddler does this "close eyes, lean in and smoulder" thing when she kisses you, and it's so cute – guess she's been watching me and Daddy!' **Zoe**

'Don't you just love the way toddlers run? When do we stop running like mad people with our arms flailing everywhere?' **Serena**

'The sweetest thing is if I hurt myself and say ouch my daughter then says, "Oh noooooooo", and holds the palm of her hands up to the sky! It just makes it all so rewarding.' **Bridget**

'I love it when he blows kisses – just the way his chubby open hand goes to his mouth and then he pulls it away. He has just associated it with "goodbye" and he does it to everyone – from the ladies in Asda to the nurses who gave him his MMR!' **Nicola**

'I love those very rare moments when she will lie in my arms and look at me as if to say, hey Mum, you're not so bad really despite your crazed eyes and stressed-up hair!' **Maxi**

'When he cuddles into my neck for no apparent reason ... I am sure he is telling me he loves me!' **Shirley**

'I love it when I go to get him out of his cot and he looks up at me with the biggest smile every time. I hate getting out of bed so that smile makes it all worthwhile for me.' **Ellie**

# Useful Resources

## Chapter One: Looking After Yourself

FlyLady
*A site that offers lessons in organising and managing your home.*
www.flylady.net


## Chapter Two: Getting Back in Shape

Body-*for*-LIFE
*A website supporting the 12-week nutrition and exercise programme for improving your body and health.*
www.bodyforlife.com


The Couch-to-5K/Cool Running
*Cool running is an online collection of information and services on running. Its Couch to 5K plan is a simple schedule to help beginners start running.*
www.coolrunning.com, www.c25k.com


The Guild of Pregnancy and Postnatal Exercise Instructors
*An organisation that teaches fitness and exercise to mothers.*
www.postnatalexercise.co.uk

Slimming World
*A slimming organisation offering unique eating plans.*
www.slimmingworld.com
0844 897 8000

Weight Watchers
*The popular weight-loss organisation with a flexible plan.*
www.weightwatchers.com
0845 607 0687

## Chapter Three: Relationships

Relate
*Relationship advice, counselling, workshops and therapy.*
www.relate.org.uk
0300 100 1234

## Chapter Four: Mums on the Move

BabyGoes2
*A site offering parents guidance on travelling with children.*
www.babygoes2.com

EHIC
*For applying for a European Health Insurance Card.*
www.ehic.org.uk
0845 605 0707

JoJo Maman Bébé
*Clothing store offering holiday and swimwear for kids.*
www.jojomamanbebe.co.uk
0871 423 5656

Little Trekkers
*Outdoor products for children, including Macpac carriers.*
www.littletrekkers.co.uk
0844 855 3242

So Baby
*Organic baby food website that offers holiday packs.*
www.so-baby.co.uk
01829 772 555

Tiny Tots Away
*A site that delivers baby shopping to your holiday destination.*
www.tinytotsaway.com

*Family-friendly hotels*

Bedruthan Steps Hotel
www.bedruthan.com
01637 860555

Luxury Family Hotels
www.luxuryfamilyhotels.co.uk

The Old Bell Hotel
www.oldbellhotel.co.uk
01666 822344

## Chapter Five: Going Back to Work or Being a Full-Time Mum

The National Childminding Association (NCMA)
*Guidance on choosing childcare.*
www.ncma.org.uk

# Contented Baby Newsletter

To learn more about the Contented Baby routines and Gina Ford's books, visit Gina's official websites at www.contentedbaby.com and www.contentedtoddler.com and sign up to receive Gina's free monthly newsletter, which is full of useful information, tips and advice as well as answers to questions about parenting issues and even a recipe or two.

You may also want to take the opportunity to become part of Gina's online community by joining one or both of the websites. As a member you'll receive a monthly online magazine with a personal message from Gina, along with a selection of the latest exclusive features on topical issues from our guest contributors and members. You'll be able to access more than 2,000 frequently asked questions about feeding, sleeping and development answered by Gina and her team, as well as many case histories not featured in the *Contented Little Baby* series of books.

www.contentedbaby.com
www.contentedtoddler.com
www.contentedbaby.com/shop-directory.htm

# Contented Baby Consultation Service

Gina offers a one-to-one personal telephone consultation service for parents who wish for specialist help in establishing healthy feeding and sleeping habits, as laid out in the Contented Baby and Toddler routine books. If you would like further details of how a personal consultation with Gina works, we would request that in the first instance you send a detailed feeding and sleeping diary for 48 hours, along with a concise summary of what you think your problem is, using the contact form on www.contentedbaby.com.

# Index

advice from others 32, 33–4
alcohol 27
Alexander Technique 25
antenatal classes 66

baby and toddler groups 66, 154
baby bags
  for car travel 83–4
  for nursery 123
  for outings 73, 78, 110, 182–3
  for plane travel 99
baby carriers 108–9
baby classes 66
baby food, on holiday 75, 76, 95–7, 111
Babyfit 22
BabyGoes2 88, 200
batch cooking 13, 93, 182
  'holiday bags' 96
bath plugs 93
Bedruthan Steps Hotel 88
bibs, disposable 92
Big Chill Festival 106–7
Body-*for*-LIFE 22, 199
boredom 1, 4–7, 15
bottle feeding
  on holiday 75, 91, 94–5, 111
  partners giving 10pm feed 9
  periods returning 58
  working mums 122–3

breastfeeding
  avoiding leaking during sex 57
  dealing with a toddler as well 184, 190, 193
  expressing milk for daycare 132
  and healthy eating 17
  involving partners 8–9, 52
  partners feeling left out 50
  possibility of pregnancy 57–8
  and uncomfortable sex 58
  at weddings 82
  working mums 119
breast pads 57
buggies
  all-weather 154–5
  and buses 79
  posture when pushing 24, 25
  sunshades 91
bus journeys 79
Bushbaby Lite carrier 108

caesareans (C-sections), and uncomfortable sex 57
calcium, in diet 17
camping 76, 106–7
car travel 83–7
  commuting with a baby 123
  long journeys 74, 85–7
celebrity mums 17, 28
childcare 137–48, 161–2